DOWNLOAD THE FREE
WORKBOOK

Don't turn another page without downloading the free *Automate Your Routines, Guarantee Your Results Workbook!*

I'm serious.

Don't do it.

Download for free at
http://www.booksbykathryn.com/ayrgyrresource

As a big "thank you" for downloading *Automate Your Routines, Guarantee Your Results*, please download the *Automate Your Routines, Guarantee Your Results Workbook* for free. This will help you to automate your morning, evening, and eating routines in no time.

And by "no time," I mean that you'll have anywhere between twenty and two hundred habits completely automated within one week.

And, considering the fact that most people set the same goals over and over again, that is pretty rad.

Please visit *http://www.booksbykathryn.com/ayrgyrresource* to download your free *Automate Your Routines, Guarantee Your Results Workbook!*

DEDICATION

To my epic parents who kindly stick with me as I am learning how to
be a real, human adult.

Contents

DOWNLOAD THE FREE WORKBOOK   2

DEDICATION   3

Introduction: "Was that really all it took to get my life in order?"   5

Chapter 1: Routine Automation vs. Habit Formation
(And Why Routine Automation Is Better)   16

Chapter 2: What Mark Zuckerberg, Steve Jobs, and Jennifer Aniston
Understand That We Don't   27

Chapter 3: Coding Is Cool (And The Secret Weapon
Behind Automating Your Routines)   34

Chapter 4: The Five-Step Formula   41

Chapter 5: Your "Why" Will Govern Your "Try"   81

Chapter 6: Automate Your Morning Routine   87

Chapter 7: Automate your Evening Routine   124

Chapter 8: Automate Your Eating Routines   146

Chapter 9: The Final Countdown   169

An Urgent Plea + Thank You? (Yes, The Question Mark Is Intentional)   174

ACKNOWLEDGMENTS   178

"WAS THAT REALLY ALL IT TOOK TO GET MY LIFE IN ORDER?"

First things first: reading is fun.

Second things second: videos are also fun.

Third things third: I made this **short video** (link in Workbook) in case you don't have time to read this wildly entertaining and amazingly engaging introduction.

Fourth things fourth: there is also the option to both read the introduction and watch the video.

Follow your heart.

Either way, I want you to think back to the last time you thought, "Oh, I love getting up in the morning when I haven't gotten enough sleep the night before!"

Or, the last time you said, "Yep, going to bed at a reasonable hour is the easiest thing I've ever done."

Oh, and this is my favorite: "Gosh, my favorite thing to do is figure out what I'm going to eat when I have four minutes and no food in my fridge!"

Um... never.

You've never said those things.

And, if you have, you're most likely delusional.

But, if you're not one of those "I love waking up when I'm tired" people - do they even exist?! - then I'm happy for you.

Why?

Because your life is about to change.

high five

In *Automate Your Routines, Guarantee Your Results,* we're going to learn how to completely automate your morning, evening, and eating routines.

And, heck - you can apply these principles to any other routine in your life to make boring, stressful, and difficult tasks become second nature.

SORRY BEYONCÉ, I NEVER WOKE UP FLAWLESS.

I used to hate getting up in the mornings.

I was also extremely bad at it.

A few summers ago, I had a job where I had to report every morning at 7:00am.

I would pretty consistently sleep through my alarm and get up between 6:46am and 6:49am, leaving me right at four minutes to put on a skirt and arrive to work six minutes late.

If you're thinking, "Wow, I bet she looked crazy every day," you would be 100% correct.

Unfortunately, my inability to function in the morning was coupled with my hatred for getting ready for bed.

Along with my hatred for actually going to bed

Preparing meals wasn't on my list of favorite things either.

"IT JUST SO HAPPENS THAT YOUR FRIEND HERE IS MOSTLY DEAD." (PRINCESS BRIDE, A TRUE CLASSIC)

There are only so many days where you can show up to work looking certifiably insane before you realize things need to change.

Alarmingly, that number of days was higher for me than it should have been.

Either way (to my immense relief), I figured out how to eliminate the things I hated from my routines.

And, with the things I couldn't eliminate (like having to get up in the mornings), I learned how to automate them so they were mindless.

I did this because honestly, I was going crazy.

And because mornings never go away.

And neither do nights.

And neither does this whole desire to eat thing.

I had to figure out how to create a system that would allow me to be consistent in my daily activities.

And, do you want to know the coolest part?

I did it. I figured it out.

Do you want to know the second coolest part?

When you automate your routines, you automate your results.

SHARING IS CARING

I've compiled all of my findings in **Automate Your Routines, Guarantee Your Results**, because honestly, it would be selfish not to share it with you.

There is a simple five-step formula to eliminate the things that you don't want to do in your routines, and to streamline the things that remain.

I'm serious.

Just five steps.

And, those five steps will immediately and drastically improve your life because, if you can learn to automate your behaviors, you - by default - can start automating your results.

Now, this five-step formula isn't just a random smattering of ideas that I thought would make a subject for a good book.

I'm not here to sell you fluff.

No one has time for that.

Instead, I am here to get you results.

I've devoured hundreds of books and articles about how to master your habits and systematize various aspects of your life.

I've researched human behavior.

I have also managed web development projects and built many websites myself, making me very familiar with computer programming, a language whose sole purpose is to automate.

The five-step formula that you will follow here is actually governed by the principles of computer programming (while combining the science of decision fatigue - more on this later), to get you the results you want faster, easier, and consistently.

"OH, THIS COULD NEVER WORK! COMPUTER PROGRAMMING IS FOR, WELL, COMPUTERS!"

I can't argue with the second portion of that statement.

But, as for the "Oh, this could never work" part, I am happy to say that you are wrong.

It was human logic that generated the language, systems, and processes that govern computer programming.

And, it is the humanness of the programming languages that reveals how we can "program" or automate our bodies and minds to do what we want them to do.

Don't believe me?

Here are some of the results I enjoyed in the first four weeks of implementing the five-step formula outlined in this book:

- I lost weight without trying
- I saved $350 on food
- I read twelve books
- I started running every day (a true triumph for anyone that knows me)
- I started forming a non-profit organization
- I increased my productivity at work fourfold
- I never felt tired once throughout the day
- And I felt immeasurably more confident in myself and the direction of my life

IMAGINE (ALL THE PEOPLE, LIVING FOR TODAY, OOH OOH, OOH OOH OOH)

Now before I delve into more details about the contents of this book, I want you to imagine a few things:

How would your days change if your morning routine was executed flawlessly?

- If you woke up on time?
- If you woke up feeling refreshed?
- If you didn't feel rushed in the morning?
- If you actually liked what you were wearing and how you looked?
- If you took your vitamins?
- If you had time to eat breakfast?
- If you meditated?
- If you exercised?
- If you had time to read before going to work?
- If you had time to make lunches for your kids?

How would your days change if your evening routine was executed flawlessly?

- If you went to bed on time?
- If you actually washed your face and whitened your teeth?
- If you read before going to bed?
- If you addressed a higher power before bed?
- If you planned for the next day?

How would your days change if you never had to stress about food?

- If you knew exactly what you were going to eat for breakfast, lunch, and dinner?
- If you didn't feel guilty about what you ate?
- If you ate consistently so you never felt hungry?
- If you had meals prepared for you so you never had to waste time cooking?

I guarantee you that if you follow the formula outlined in this book, your life will be completely different.

And by "completely different," I mean-

- more productive
- more controlled
- less stressful
- a more clear mind (resulting in greater creativity and spontaneity)
- more optimistic
- and more confident.

THIS IS BETTER THAN OREOS AND PEANUT BUTTER (WHICH IS REALLY SAYING SOMETHING).

Here is what to look forward to in *Automate Your Routines, Guarantee Your Results,* should you make the wise* decision to keep reading:

(*Note: "wise" can be substituted with "obvious" or "insanely intelligent")

● **You will automate your AM, PM, and eating routines**

When you decide to automate your routines, you only have to make the decision once. It's kind of like automatic bill pay. Once you go onto your bank's website and set it up (decide one time), it's done! Your bills will automatically be paid for the rest of forever!

Well, that's what we're going to do with your behaviors. We're going to show you how to get results by only choosing once.

● **Boring, stressful, and difficult parts of your routines will become second nature.**

We're talking complete autopilot, people.

● **Your time will be liberated.**

By automating your routines, you'll free the time that is currently captive (because you're doing things last minute, or facing the consequences of not doing them at all).

● **You will erase your bad habits.**

I'll show you how to literally write these out of your life.

● **And you'll free up your brain power like Steve Jobs (a master of automation) to focus on more "take-over-the-world" type ventures.**

As a side note, Steve Jobs changed the world forever, was brilliant, and was crazy rich.

So, if that's not enough to pull you in, then that's quite unfortunate for the both of us.

● Unfortunate for you because you're maybe, probably...how do I say this...boring.

● Unfortunate for me because you will most likely not read this book.

I've digressed.

11

I recognize that the promises mentioned above are some pretty hefty promises.

But, I am confident in promising them because I've seen this process work.

IT'S ABOUT TO GET PERSONAL.

Here's a blunt warning of what will happen if you decide to not read and apply the principles in this book -

I WILL HUNT YOU DOWN IN YOUR SLEEP.

Just kidding.

(Maybe?)

Nah, here's the real warning: your life will be a crazy, sporadic, and exhausting mess.

In case you don't believe me, here is further evidence of that warning, delivered in a series of alarmingly personal (and altogether pathetic) fun facts:

- **Fun fact #1:** I used to be anemic.
- **Fun fact #2:** Being anemic means you're extremely iron deficient.
- **Fun fact #3:** It's common to be addicted to eating ice and/or eating sidewalk chalk when you're anemic.
- **Fun fact #4:** Yes, you read that right: ice and/or sidewalk chalk.
- **Fun fact #5:** Gratefully (so gratefully), I was addicted to ice, not sidewalk chalk.

(For all you sidewalk chalk chomping anemics out there, I hear Smarties are a good substitute.)

Before you go feeling sorry for me as the college freak who had to do all of her studying in the campus food court because she needed to be near the ice machine every second of every day, well, don't feel sorry for me.

Being anemic was entirely my fault.

I had no structure in my life.

Which meant I went to bed at the craziest, most random times.

And I woke up at the craziest, most random times.

And, I ate at the craziest, most random times.

That meant that I would pretty regularly consume Wheat Thins, string cheese, and root beer from the vending machine for dinner.

That "meal" has a total of 4% of your recommended daily iron.

Yeah, being anemic was totally my fault.

ENOUGH IS ENOUGH.

Fast forward six years.

I am no longer anemic.

I know, I know. I'm happy for me too.

But, until a while ago, I still was awful at waking up.

And going to bed.

And eating at normal times, eating healthy foods, and eating at all.

I finally thought, "Enough is enough! I am now in the second quarter of my life. I will not be ruled by my pathetic, snooze-button-addicted, inconsistent self!"

Now, I wasn't unaccomplished.

In fact, in the year prior, I graduated from college with a Bachelor of Arts degree and two business minors, I was working a full-time job, I launched an online course for my business, I met some significant, high-performers, and I dated some great people.

But, I was still plagued by my inconsistencies.

In case you haven't already gathered, I am a very passionate person.

Shocker, I know.

It was pretty typical for me to give myself to a project - ditching any plans or people to finish it.

I would stay up late, keep awful hours, and put my personal well-being on the backburner to accomplish what I needed.

My productivity was so sporadic.

My mind was exhausted.

If new ideas came to me, I would suppress them because I was afraid of how derailed my life would become if I tried to turn any idea into a reality.

My body was deteriorating.

Remember my bout with anemia? I also felt so unhealthy, I had awful sleep hours, and I would get sick all the time.

Also, my social life was inconsistent.

Because I couldn't hold any sort of routine, there would be days when I still wasn't ready for the day at 6:00pm.

So, if a friend called me to hang out or go to dinner, I would make up some excuse as to why I couldn't go, when in reality, I was embarrassed that it was 6:00pm and I was still in my pajamas.

Moral of the story: crazy and sporadic messes remain crazy and sporadic messes until they choose to change.

"WAS THIS REALLY ALL IT TOOK TO GET MY LIFE IN ORDER?"

I was very serious about my declaration, "Enough is enough!"

I thought, "What could happen if I automated my morning, evening, and eating routines so that they were no longer a source of annoyance?"

"What could happen if I was in complete control of the things that stressed me out?"

"What could happen if I eliminated my bad habits?"

"What could happen if I liberated my time to focus on things I actually wanted to do?"

Well, I'm sure you could see this coming (as I've said it before), but I've got some great news for you: I figured it out.

I figured out how to do *all* of it.

And, it's all here for you to learn, implement, and then watch your life change like magic.

Honestly, the results are nearly immediate.

Freaky fast.

I kept thinking, "Was this really all it took to get my life in order?"

If you follow the five-step formula outlined in this book, I promise that you'll be saying the same thing: "Was this really all it took to get my life in order?"

Alright, alright! I'll stop talking.

Automate your morning, evening, and eating routines to eliminate your bad habits, liberate your time, and start focusing on what is most important to you.

Flip the page to start learning how.

Consider this overly sassy (but, don't pretend like you weren't entertained) introduction complete.

CHAPTER 1:

ROUTINE AUTOMATION VS. HABIT FORMATION (AND WHY ROUTINE AUTOMATION IS BETTER)

"How in the world is Automate Your Routines, Guarantee Your Results going to be different from every other book I've read on habit formation?"

I'm glad you asked.

And, I'm happy to tell you.

I'M IN LOVE, I'M IN LOVE, AND I DON'T CARE WHO KNOWS IT!

But first, it's probably important to tell you that I'm in love with an Indian man who is eight years older than me.

He has no idea.

Also, I've never met him.

Here's what happened: a few years ago, I became obsessed with the entrepreneur lifestyle.

I started following (aka stalking) people like Tim Ferris, James Altucher, and Seth Godin. I literally devoured everything that they published.

(Note: It's weird feeling so close to people who have no idea you exist.)

The first exposure I had to this type of entrepreneur content was through my soul mate, a man amongst men - Ramit Sethi.

(I hope more than anything he is reading this book. Probably because we need to be in love. Or, at least be friends. Okay fine, I'll settle for a conversation over dinner.)

I absolutely adore him for the principles that he taught me.

For years, my brother recommended that I read a book of Ramit's called, *I Will Teach You to Be Rich.*

I finally decided to read it.

In the book, Ramit outlines how you can completely take control of your financial life, and do it in a way that is simple and painless.

He talks about how to automate your savings, your investing, your credit building, and how to get out of debt.

The content of the book is priceless, and the way he delivers the content is refreshingly terrifying.

"Terrifying?"

Yes, terrifying.

The man holds nothing back. If he thinks you're an idiot, he'll tell you that you're an idiot. If he thinks you're brilliant, he'll tell you that you're brilliant. If he knows a system will work, he'll tell you exactly what you need to do to make it happen.

Now, the way that he tells you to take control of your financial life is to automate it.

"I am going to teach you how to build an automated system to handle your money so that you can focus on the bigger picture," Ramit said. "Like, using the time saved to make more money."

When I read this as a young, 20-year-old girl, I was completely intimidated by the financial world.

To be honest, I was intimidated by things that I didn't know about (what the heck was a Roth IRA account?!), and I almost felt embarrassed to ask for help.

As I read Ramit's book, I started to see immediate results in my life. Honestly, within a few weeks, I had done things that my formerly naive self would have never done, like start regularly investing money.

All of a sudden, I was able to see the brilliance behind automation in the finance world.

And, this is why I am in love with Ramit.

He showed me the power of automation.

A WHOLE NEW WORLD (DON'T YOU DARE CLOSE YOUR EYES).

As I've matured, I've started to apply the principles of automation to different areas of my life.

These are some of the results:

1. I have started building a non-profit.
2. I work remotely.
3. I run an online business.
4. I feel confident that I can finish whatever project I start.
5. And, mostly, I feel free.

Power came into my life when I learned that I could automate everything that was boring, stressful, and difficult.

IT'S AUTOMATIC, SYSTEMATIC, HYDROMATIC.

Now, before we go further, it's important to understand what automation is.

When something is automatic, it "works by itself with little or no direct human control." It is also something that is done "without conscious thought."

That element of doing things without "conscious thought," especially the things that I hated most (remember my morning, evening, and eating routine angst from the introduction?), was exactly what I desired.

I then hoped to allocate those "conscious" thoughts to things that I wanted to focus on, whether they be other business opportunities, my relationships, or simply being present wherever I was.

Now, people in the industrial world understand the power of automation. After all, anything that is manufactured is automated.

As mentioned before, the finance world also understands automation. With things like automatic bill pay, automatic savings, and automatic investing, keeping your finances in check has never been easier.

The technological world is also brilliant at the automation process. There are new software programs being released daily, consisting of code that will automate even the most impossible of tasks.

But, where we really underutilize the power of automation is in our behaviors.

PLAY-DOH IS CREEPY, BUT DOMINOS ARE FUN.

"But, what about habits?" you say. "There's been like a million and a half books written about habits!"

You are correct.

Yay, you get a gold star.

But, there is a difference between habit formation and routine automation.

And, it's your ignorance of this difference that results in you making the same New Year's resolutions every year.

WHY HABIT FORMATION IS LIKE PLAY-DOH.

Let's break down each word in the phrase "habit formation."

- **Habit (n.):** a settled or regular tendency or practice, especially one that is hard to give up.
- **Formation (v.):** the action of configuring something.

Here's what I see: a habit is one practice. Formation occurs after action.

Somehow, my mind skips to Play-doh when I hear the word formation.

Take a second and think about what it's like to play with Play-doh.

Let's pretend that with your Play-doh, you're trying to build a person.

19

You have to mold the arms, make a circle for a head, and make the legs solid enough to hold up the torso.

Unfortunately, unless you're a Play-doh expert (which, if you are, email me), every person you try to make out of Play-doh resembles a mutated clown with big eyes and a huge, red mouth. And, it even droops over because the dough isn't strong enough to stand on its own.

And, instead of creating a person, you've unintentionally created a zombie.

I have nightmares about things like that.

Once your person/zombie starts falling forward, you have to reshape it, reposition it, and stand it upright again.

The act of forming requires a lot of work. A lot of continuous work.

That makes me tired just thinking about it.

It makes me want to give up.

But, routine automation is different.

THREE CHEERS FOR DOMINOS (THE GAME, NOT THE PIZZA).

Let's look at these words individually.

Routine automation

- **Routine (n.):** a sequence of actions regularly followed; a fixed program
- **Automation (v.) (we looked at this earlier):** something done by itself, or with little human control; without conscious thought

Routines are a series of actions. A series. Meaning more than one.

Automation is something that you only have to choose to do once.

Since we just used Play-doh as an example for habit formation, let's stick with the childhood toys and use dominos to explore the power of routine automation.

When dominos are set up one next to another, they create a pattern.

Then, once they've all been lined up, the domino at the beginning of the line is pushed, only to knock over the next domino, which knocks over the next domino, which knocks over the next domino.

Though dominos take a little time to set up, once you push over the first domino, the remaining dominos fall over automatically.

You do not have to manually push over each individual domino.

That is how routine automation works.

You have to do a little work up front by setting up the dominos, but once it's complete, the routine can be automated flawlessly and automatically.

So, you can either form one habit at a time with the creepy zombie Play-doh people or you can automate an entire routine by acting once - flick the first domino in the pattern.

(To see a short video that shows this, see the link in your Workbook.)

DEAR HATERS, I UNDERSTAND YOU.

If you're skeptical, let's explore some downfalls associated with habit formation.

The first major problem with forming habits is that it requires extended periods of time.

There is a brilliant professor at Stanford named BJ Fogg. He runs a program called "Tiny Habits."

Within this program, he informs that if you want someone to develop the habit of flossing, simply telling them to floss every day isn't going to do it.

Instead, you need to tell people to floss one tooth at a time. Then, once they've mastered that, you must tell them to floss two teeth, and then three, and so on.

He then says that you should link new habits to pre-existing habits, one addition at a time.

A quick example of this is from my father.

My dad is a great dad. I mean, really exceptional.

And, he has eight kids.

He wanted to increase both the amount and quality of communication he had with his children, especially those that had moved out of the house.

So, he created a tiny habit (i.e. send one, quick text to each child at the end of the day) which he linked to a pre-existing habit (i.e. charging his phone).

Now, every night when he charges his phone, he immediately texts all of his children.

As the recipient of his texts, I absolutely love it.

BJ Fogg's method of habit formation works. In fact, it's brilliant.

But, it's slow. It's tedious. It requires one tiny action, built on another tiny action, over a very extended period of time.

Other habit formation experts, including Charles Duhigg and James Clear also have incredible proven tactics to develop habits.

But, they all require so much time.

With these systems, you have to keep tweaking and refining, one minuscule habit at a time.

This process of formation requires an extended devotion of time and effort, something that doesn't bode well for typical human behavior.

The second major problem with forming habits is that it is fueled by motivation.

Typical human behavior looks like this:

1. Watch Netflix.
2. "Ugh, I hate myself."
3. Watch more Netflix.
4. "No, I seriously hate myself."
5. Fail test/don't show up for work/something bad happens because you keep not changing your habits.
6. "Okay, if I don't change, I'm doomed."
7. "Ugh, I hate myself."
8. Google, "How do I stop my addiction to Netflix?"
9. Find a blog article.
10. Feel inspired.
11. Get pumped!
12. Follow this surge of motivation to try and build one habit at a time.
13. Goes great for two days.
14. Motivation dies.
15. It's too hard to think about adding on another habit.
16. Too tired.
17. Too hard.
18. Go back to Netflix.
19. Follow this same process for the next fifty years until you're dead.
20. Never actually change.
21. Netflix wins.

This process relies on motivation, or inspiration.

But, motivation and inspiration are fleeting.

They don't show up every day.

So, what will you do when you think, "I don't feel like working out?"

Or, what will you do if you think, "I don't want to eat healthy today?"

If your routines are governed by motivation, then I guarantee you won't work out, and you won't eat healthily.

You'll slip back into your old routines, and start steps 1-21 all over again. You'll always make the same goals and you'll always fail to reach them.

Also - how's this for a downer? - not only is motivation fleeting, but the amount of willpower you have is limited.

WHEN ALL YOU WANT IS FOR YOUR WILLPOWER TO LOOK LIKE ARNOLD SCHWARZENEGGER.

Willpower works just like a muscle. When you expend your willpower energy, the muscle gets tired, and you eventually have to rest.

If you've read any productivity blog of any form, people are always screaming at you to preserve your willpower, or "conscious thought," for things that are most important.

For example, we're often advised, "Do not check your email first thing in the morning!"

Why?

Chandler Bolt, an author and successful entrepreneur, explained in his book *The Productive Person*, that when you start your day by reading email or scrolling through social media, you are immediately entering into a reactive mode, rather than a proactive mode.

And, it is insanely difficult to switch from doing reactive tasks to proactive tasks.

To clarify, let's look at the difference between reactive tasks and proactive tasks.

Examples of reactive tasks:

- **You read an email in the morning that says,**

Hey Jon,

It looks like my doctor's appointment is going to be during our meeting time.

When can we reschedule?

When you respond, you are reacting to what your co-worker said.

Another example of a reactive task:

- **You are scrolling through Facebook in the morning and you see that your mom has posted a video of a Disney songs mashup.**

Now, I'll be honest: a Disney songs mashup is good for the soul every once in a while.

But, watching it right when you wake up is the absolute worst thing to do!

Why?

Because you are *reacting.* You are allowing someone else (in this case, the mashup video) to determine what happens with your time.

If you constantly choose to enter into a reacting mode, you will not be successful.

Instead, you will help other people to become successful because you will always do what people tell you to do (whether that's watching their YouTube video, liking their post, adhering to their email, or switching your schedule).

But you, yourself, will never achieve success.

Your brain power, or your "conscious thought" is limited.

So, if you waste your brain power on reactive tasks, or even tasks that you hate (showering, exercising, planning out meals, etc.), you will never have the energy to do proactive projects.

25

You will never have the energy to achieve your own success.

So, the urgent plea you hear from within yourself to automate your routines is an authentic one.

Building one habit at a time is not a terrible idea. But, it is clearly inferior to automating routines.

Remember, when you form a habit, you are taking time and extended effort to build one, new, tiny action.

When you automate routines, you choose once to create a series of hundreds of actions.

If you're smart, you'll choose the "automate routine" plan instead of wasting your time trying to form a habit that doesn't turn into a routine.

And now that we understand what routine automation is, let's figure out how to make it happen.

The next chapter will show you how.

CHAPTER 2:

WHAT MARK ZUCKERBERG, STEVE JOBS, AND JENNIFER ANISTON UNDERSTAND THAT WE DON'T

Before we jump into the nitty gritty of routine automation, let's look at some people who have mastered the process.

HEY MARK.

To start, let's explore the life of **Mark Zuckerberg,** the founder of Facebook.

If you have watched him in any public appearance over the last five years, you will most likely have noticed that he always wears the same outfit: a pair of jeans, a gray t-shirt, and (if he's feeling fancy) a black, zip-up hoodie.

Hawt.

He often gets teased for this appearance. In fact, in a public Q&A, he was playfully poked about his wardrobe choices.

Interestingly, Zuckerberg responded very seriously: "I really want to clear my life to make it so that I have to make as few decisions as possible about anything except how to best serve this community."

Apparently he has multiples of each part of his outfit so that the decision to choose what to wear doesn't consume his time or energy.

He continued by saying, "I'm in this really lucky position, where I get to wake up every day and help serve more than a billion people. And, I feel like I'm not doing my job if I spend any of my energy on things that are silly or frivolous about my life."

For him, choosing what to wear was a silly and frivolous thing. So, what did he do? He eliminated options and automated the process of getting ready every day.

THE MAN, THE MYTH, THE LEGEND.

Let's now dissect the life of **Steve Jobs,** another incredible human.

Before anything else is said about Steve Jobs, I want you to imagine him.

What is he wearing?

(Wait for it...)

A black turtleneck.

Why is he wearing that? Because that's all he ever wore!

Here's how his singular outfit choice came about:

In the early 1980s, Jobs was spending time with the chairman of Sony. Jobs found out that in Sony's factory, the employees all wore the same uniforms as a way to bond with one another and to the company.

Jobs thought that was a brilliant idea.

So, he worked closely with a famous designer to create a uniform for all Apple employees. The uniform was a jacket of rip-stop nylon with sleeves that could unzip to make it into a vest.

Jobs said, "I came back with samples and told everyone [at Apple] that it would be great if we would all wear these vests. Oh man, did I get booed off the stage. Everybody hated the idea."

Interestingly, Job's initial objective for creating these uniforms wasn't for simplicity, but because he wanted to bond the employees to each other and the company.

Either way, as a result of the process, Jobs began to like the idea of having a uniform for himself.

Why?

He wanted a uniform because of its daily convenience.

So, he had the designer make him one hundred black turtlenecks.

For convenience, Jobs eliminated the choice of what to wear every day.

The desire for easy decisions in his life - for automating behaviors - even expanded to the decor of his home.

This meant that the decor of his home was essentially non-existent.

He had a chest of drawers, a mattress in his bedroom, a card table, and some folding chairs for when he had guests.

His wife remarked, "We spoke about furniture in theory for eight years. We spent a lot of time asking ourselves, 'What is the purpose of a sofa?'"

He did not want to clutter his life with things that would disable him to think clearly or that would require his limited conscious thought.

Jobs' intentional consideration of what required his contribution allowed him to both simplify and automate.

NEWSFLASH: ROSS WASN'T RACHEL'S LOBSTER...SALAD WAS.

Jennifer Aniston is an extremely popular actress both in movies and television.

In an interview with Courtney Cox, Jennifer Aniston's former co-star on the TV sitcom *Friends,* Cox said, "Jennifer...and I ate lunch together every single day for 10 years. We always had the same thing - a Cobb salad."

Let's talk about that - the same salad, every day, for ten years! That's 3,650 Cobb salads!

Why did they do it? They did it because they knew it was healthy, and by eating the same thing every day, they could easily manage what was going into their body. They didn't have to stress about finding food that was not going to hinder their figure.

Aniston had found a solution, and she stuck with it.

Zuckerberg, Jobs, and Aniston all understood and applied the basics of something called "decision fatigue."

Decision fatigue "refers to the deteriorating quality of decisions made by an individual, after a long session of decision making."

Essentially, the more decisions you make, the worse you get at making decisions.

So, what did Zuckerberg, Jobs, and Aniston do? They made a decision of what they were going to wear/eat, and then they never chose again.

They enhanced their decision-making ability by not allowing it to become "fatigued" with non-vital concerns.

And, by choosing the same things, every day, the decision became mindless, required no conscious thought, and ultimately became automated.

TELL ME MORE, TELL ME MORE, LIKE DOES HE HAVE A CAR.

There are many more impactful people who have powerful, consistent, and automated routines.

Tony Robbins is a self-help writer and a motivational speaker. Every morning he starts his day with an "Hour of Power," where he engages in visualizations and consumes motivational words and stories.

Barack Obama starts every day with a 6:45am workout, then reads the newspaper, has breakfast with his family, and starts his work day just before 9:00am.

Franz Kafka, the famous author, had an interesting set of routines, though they were consistent and automated.

Kafka worked for an insurance institute from 8:30am to 2:30pm. He would then eat lunch until 3:30pm, and sleep until 7:30pm. Then, he would exercise and eat with his family. He would then write from 11:00pm until 2:00am in the morning.

Marilyn Monroe, the famous actress, was said to have automated her eating routine. She said, "Before I take my morning shower, I start warming a cup of milk on the hot plate I keep in my hotel room. When it's hot, I break two raw eggs into the milk, whip them up with a fork, and drink them while I'm dressing. I supplement this with a multivitamin pill, and I doubt if any doctor would recommend a more nourishing breakfast for a working girl in a hurry."

If we look at these people - **Mark Zuckerberg, Steve Jobs, Jennifer Aniston, Tony Robbins, Barack Obama, Franz Kafka,** and **Marilyn Monroe** - they all had significantly different responsibilities.

But each of their roles required amazingly unique creativity and abnormally high levels of productivity.

You will notice that each of them had their own routines.

You will also notice that their routines were consistent and automated.

You will also notice that the results of these routines have benefited them monetarily, emotionally, physically, and professionally.

Most importantly, these automated routines allowed them all to be great thinkers and consistent implementers of ideas.

YOU'RE ONTO SOMETHING HERE.

Before I understood the power of automating routines, and how to automate routines, my life was a cleverly disguised mess.

Even though I may have seemed like I was on top of things, I was all over the place.

I couldn't do anything consistently, including waking up on time, getting ready for the day, taking vitamins, eating any semblance of a healthy meal, getting enough sleep, going to bed at a reasonable hour, studying, reading...anything!

My efforts were sporadic and exhausting.

So, I looked at the areas of my life that were under control: my finances.

Why were my finances under control? Because I had automated them.

I thought, "How could I use the same principles that I use to automate my finances to automate my routines?"

At the time of writing this book, if you type in "how to automate" into Google, three articles will appear at the top:

1.   How to automate time-consuming tasks with code

2.   Automate boring stuff with Python

3.   10 great tools to automate and outsource your work (referring to different SaaS's, or software as a services)

Anytime the word automation arises, it is linked to coding (or computer programming)!

I thought, "Oh my gosh, that's how I can automate my routines!   I'll code them!"

Now, I fully recognize that we can't import some Javascript or Python (these are programming languages, for you non-techies out there) into your brain to make you do certain things.

But, we can follow similar principles that coders use to rewire your brain. This rewiring will allow you to create and complete your ideal routines (we'll cover this in the next chapter).

YOU'VE GOT TO BE KIDDING ME, RIGHT?

Nope, not kidding.

Through the principles of coding, we are going to teach your brain new mindsets that allow the routines you create to become instincts.

We're also going to combine the science of coding with the principles of decision fatigue to eliminate unnecessary choices and road bumps.

We'll make sure to automate the things that are annoying, boring, and difficult.

If you're tempted to skip out on this because the words "coding" and "programming" seem nerdy and complicated, don't!

I've broken it down so that you can easily apply the necessary principles to automate your morning, evening, and eating routines.

Also, remember that programmers have mastered the code to automation (something that you need).

You'll find out how to start the process of creating your routines in the next chapter.

You're welcome.

(Also, don't hate on the geeky coders. They're people, too.)

CHAPTER 3:

CODING IS COOL (AND THE SECRET WEAPON BEHIND AUTOMATING YOUR ROUTINES)

Coding is cool.

I wish I had a shirt that said that. (Hint, hint.)

By the end of this chapter, you are going to understand why coding is so cool, and how learning the basics of coding (we're talking the very basics) are essential to automating your routines.

"Wait, you're going to try to convince me that coding is cool?"

Why yes, and I'm going to do it successfully.

Intrigued?

WHAT IS CODING?

Coding is devising a list of steps that instruct a computer what it should do to solve a specific problem.

These steps are described as either processes or procedures.

THE DIFFERENCE BETWEEN PROCESSES AND PROCEDURES.

It is important to understand the difference between processes and procedures.

A process is known as the "big picture."

To give an example of a process, imagine that you type "directions from Salt Lake City to Denver" into Google.

A map that shows a highlighted pathway from Salt Lake City to Denver will appear.

That overhead map, or the "big picture" outline, could be described as the "process" to get from Salt Lake City to Denver.

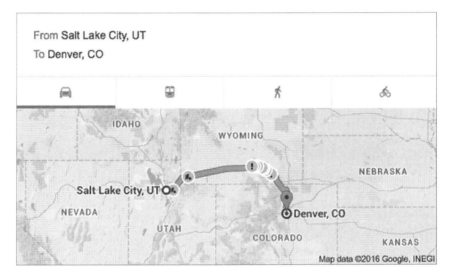

A procedure is a little different.

A procedure is a series of actions conducted in a certain order.

To go along with our map example, the procedure to get from Salt Lake City to Denver would be

1. Get on I-15S/I-80E.

2. Follow I-80E to US-287. Take exit 313 from I-80E.

3. Get on I-25S in Larimer County.

4. Etc.

The procedure outlines exact steps: what roads to drive on, how long to drive on them, and how long each segment of the drive will take.

> Get on I-15 S/I-80 E from 400 South/University Blvd

4 min (1.6 mi)

> Follow I-80 E to US-287 S/S 3rd St in Laramie. Take exit 313 from I-80 E

5 h 40 min (389 mi)

> Get on I-25 S in Larimer County

59 min (57.8 mi)

> Follow I-25 S to US-287 S/US-40 E/W Colfax Ave in Denver. Take exit 210A from I-25 S

1 h 3 min (71.0 mi)

By understanding processes and procedures, coders are able to identify pressing problems, and then create procedures (or exact steps) to solve them.

If you're still trying to wrap your mind around coding, know that it can be likened to dealing with a smart aleck kid. They don't do what you want them to do, they do what you tell them to do.

For example, if you instructed a smart aleck kid to hop into the bathtub, he would jump in with his clothes on, no water running.

Later, when you went to check on him, you would find the boy still dirty, sitting in the bathtub.

You might ask, "Why aren't you bathed?!"

"Well," the child would respond, "you never told me to bathe. You only told me to hop in the bathtub."

To avoid the faux pas described (or a computer program that doesn't work), programmers must write processes that are exact and procedures that are specific. This ensures that the programs will not only work, but also that they won't "misbehave" or do something unwanted.

Now, don't forget, coding is cool. And, understanding the basics of coding is required for routine automation.

CODING SCHOOLS ARE ALL THE RAGE.

Let's outline more specific reasons as to why coding is cool.

First, it is very challenging.

Problems are identified, and solutions are created. It is rewarding to see the results in action.

Secondly, coding is cool because it is needed.

There are coding schools being built all over the world.

There are also many coding bootcamps - a high-intensity learning environment where people prepare themselves to land an entry-level web developer job in just three to six months.

To lure even more people to code, there are many schools that will only accept women or minorities.

There are also programs that only require you to pay tuition if you are offered a job upon graduation of their program.

There is a school in Utah Valley, called DevMountain, that will pay for your housing if you're a full-time student.

It is also interesting to note that my seventh-grade sister is being taught beginning concepts of coding in her middle school classes.

The world needs coders!

To be honest, I don't necessarily believe that the primary benefit of increasing the number of coders in the world is having a larger list of people who can perfectly code in Python, C++, or JavaScript (these are different programming languages, like Spanish or German).

Rather, it is becoming apparent that the principles that govern coding contain the present and future principles of problem solving.

Employers are craving individuals who can quickly and accurately identify problems and then design processes and procedures to solve those problems.

Anything from organizing globally impactful issues to eliminating mundane tasks can be done via coding.

Can you now see why, even if you never actually learn how to code, understanding the principles of coding is essential?!

CODING MAKES EVERYTHING BETTER.

Coding transforms the way you think, making coding (you guessed it) cool.

There is a man named Seymour Papert, who, in his book called **Mindstorms** said, "A deep understanding of programming, in particular the notions of successive decomposition as a mode of analysis and debugging of trial solutions, results in significant educational benefits in many domains of discourse, including those unrelated to computers and information technology per se."

Programmer Donald Knuth said, "It has been said that a person does not really understand something until he teaches it to someone else. Actually a person does not really understand something until teaching it to a computer, i.e., express it as an algorithm" ("American Mathematical Monthly," 81).

But, it was James P. Hogan, in **Mind Matters**, that brilliantly summarized the essential benefits of coding:

"Computers have proven immensely effective as aids to clear thinking. Muddled and half-baked ideas have sometimes survived for centuries because luminaries have deluded themselves as much as their followers or because lesser lights, fearing ridicule, couldn't summon up the nerve to admit that they didn't know what the Master was talking about. A test as near foolproof as one could get of whether you understand something as well as you think is to express it as a computer program and then see if the program does what it is supposed to do. Computers are not sycophants and won't make enthusiastic noises to ensure their promotion or camouflage what they don't know. What you get is what you said."

It takes some initial time to learn the principles of coding, but when they are applied to any area of your life (whether professionally, in relationships, or in routine automation), they will take shape.

Coding can be used to identify problems, design solutions, execute programs, and then debug them so they are not only usable and effective, but produce automatic results.

SAY "HELLO" TO MY LITTLE FRIEND.

To understand just how epic and real these automatic results can be, I want to tell you about something called passive income.

Now, I read a lot. A lot of books, a lot of blogs, a lot of articles.

The primary content of these articles centers around productivity, online business, and entrepreneurship.

In my studies, I have learned a lot about passive income.

I immediately became obsessed with this idea of passive income.

Passive income is "an income received on a regular basis, with little effort required to maintain it."

Little effort required to maintain it?

Um, yes please.

You will see that it says that it requires little effort to "maintain" it, not necessarily to "create" it.

Passive income requires a lot of work up front, which you are then paid for later.

A simple example is book writing.

Let's look at Stephen Covey's book, *Seven Habits of Highly Effective People.*

Steven Covey published the book in 1989, and had to do a lot of work to research, write, and make it available to the public.

But, once he did, he was done! The book was written!

He wrote it once, it's on sale forever, and even though he wrote the book nearly thirty years ago, he is still making money from it! It continues to be a bestseller!

Here is another example: one of my girlfriends had a medium-sized role in the Disney film, **High School Musical 2.** She was sixteen years old at the time of the filming, and the movie has been out for nearly ten years.

Now, as a twenty-five year old woman, she is still receiving royalty checks from that movie.

Coding, just like passive income, requires a degree of work up front, but the results are long lasting.

If you frontload the work then the program will run on its own, allowing you to reap the results automatically.

Additionally, if a new idea strikes and you realize that you want to update your program, all you have to do is apply tiny tweaks.

My obsession with frontloading the work and then reaping automatic results later (as is the case with coding and passive income), led me to successfully apply these principles to automate routines and behaviors.

The frustration with habit formation (a process that can be tedious and time consuming), now requires only one session of front loading the work and then, it's done!

And, as a little lass who lives a routine- and results-automated life, I can tell you that the brilliant minds who devised coding actually created principles that can automate any area of your life.

THIS. IS. A. BIG. DEAL.

Now that you understand why coding is cool (and the power that its governing principles can have in your life), flip the page to learn the exact formula to make routine automation a reality for you!

CHAPTER 4:

THE FIVE-STEP FORMULA

I know we just talked about coding.

But, we're going to talk about it again.

Why?

1. Because coding is cool (stop fighting it).

2. And secondly, the principles of coding are what are going to help you to automate your routines.

By learning the basics of coding, you will be able to conquer the drudgery of habit formation and create lasting, automatic routines.

Here's a quick summary of what is going to happen in this chapter:

- We are going to learn the five-step formula of how to apply the process of coding, or programming, more extensively to our routines.

- As a part of this formula, we'll implement the principles behind decision fatigue, ultimately eliminating unnecessary or redundant choices.

A BIRD'S EYE VIEW.

I'm going to give you an overview of how to become Steve Jobs-esque (to whatever degree of black turtleneck that you desire).

Pay attention to the word "overview" above.

The intention of this chapter is to help you get your bearings. That way, when we automate your morning, evening, and eating routines in the following chapters, the process is familiar and painless.

As a fair warning, you will feel inspired to start right away!

And I can't stop you.

But here is my official recommendation for how to navigate this chapter:

- Skim through it.
- Pay attention to new ideas that come to you!
- Quickly jot the ideas down, but don't stop reading!

Get your feet wet, start to understand the process, and then in the next chapter, we're going to start generating the results you want by creating your own automated routines.

With that said, here's the five-step formula we will follow to automate our routines:

1. **Define the problem**
2. **Design a solution**
3. **Create your program**
4. **Test your program**
5. **Document your program**

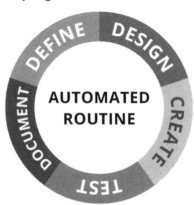

That's it!

If this formula is followed, then your routines will be:

- Perfectly constructed
- Saturated with easy-to-follow procedures
- Completely debugged
- Painless to follow
- And constantly generating automated results

Not a bad gig, eh?

Let's dissect each part.

(Remember, simply skim through this section. We're just orienting ourselves here.)

1. DEFINE THE PROBLEM

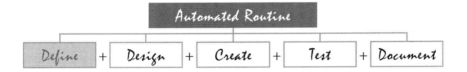

The first thing we need to do is define the problem.

A "problem" can be categorized as anything that is less convenient than you desire.

A problem includes anything that is stressful, boring, or difficult to do.

In the coding world, a problem could be any of the following:

- **Example 1:** I keep missing important emails from particular clients.
- **Example 2:** I cannot convert an MP4 file to an MP3 file.
- **Example 3:** I cannot sync my Evernote with my Google Drive as easily as I'd like.

Now, in the routine automation world, a problem could look like any of the following:

- **Example 1**: I cannot wake up on time.
- **Example 2:** I spend too much time on Facebook.
- **Example 3**: I spend too much money eating out.

In future chapters, we will explore and define problems in your life that are preventing you from being as successful, productive, or free as you would like.

We will do that by answering questions like:

1. What are activities that distract you from completing the task at hand?
2. When do you find yourself bored?
3. What are recurring events or responsibilities that leave you stressed?
4. What is the most difficult part of your day?
5. What, if eliminated, would make your day significantly better?

2. DESIGN A SOLUTION

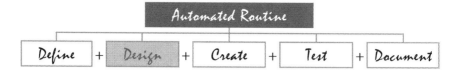

The next part of the formula is to design a solution.

Denzel Washington, the accomplished actor, said, "Dreams without goals remain dreams...and fuel disappointment."

Step two of the formula - designing a solution - requires that you draft a perfect routine.

WHEN I SAY "PERFECT," I REALLY MEAN "PERFECT."

With the intention of eliminating all of the problems you identified in step one, "designing a solution" consists of answering the question, "If I had all the time, all the willpower, all of the money, and all the resources in the world, what would I want my perfect morning/evening/eating routine to look like?"

Once your perfect routine has been drafted, we'll work in step three to make it become a reality.

I was introduced to this concept of creating the perfect solution and then implementing it as closely as possible by my older brother.

In 2009, he served a mission for our church.

As part of his missionary work, he and his companion needed to find people to who wanted to learn more about God.

They decided to try and find one hundred new people to teach within one day.

Compared to his past results and results of other missionaries around him, one hundred new people was an absurdly ambitious goal.

But, he and his companion were determined.

How did they make it happen?

They designed a solution as if they had all of the people, resources, social skills, and money that they would ever need.

After they designed this solution, they went back through and determined which things were possible and which things they would need to modify.

If it were absolutely necessary that they modify something (if it was deemed literally impossible), they would then ask the question, "What would be the next best thing?"

They continued this process, going through each element of their design and either determining it possible, or refining it to become the next best thing.

45

They then implemented their plan.

By the end of the day, they found more than sixty new people to teach.

Sixty new people was not one hundred, but it was still fifty-eight more than the amount of people they typically found in one day.

Thus, their efforts were deemed extremely successful.

When they launched this process again the next time, with only a day's worth of experience under their belt, they were able to achieve even greater success.

I remember when my brother shared this experience with me.

I began to think, "What would happen if I first sought to create things with the ideal output in mind?"

It seemed as though I had been trying to "work up to things," rather than work to create what I really wanted.

So many areas of my life have achieved significantly higher, and more rapid success, by altering my process of designing solutions.

TELL ME WHATCHA WANT, WHATCHA REALLY, REALLY WANT.

Here's another example of how I apply this thinking in my life.

Because of my age and demographic, I meet a lot of people who are still in college or who are working at their first job.

Often times, I'll ask them, "What is your dream job?"

Depressingly often, they'll either say they have -

1. No idea

2. Or, they'll start to describe their current job (or some version of it).

Sadly, and most likely, they're lying to me.

And they're lying to themselves.

If they were being extremely honest with themselves, their entry-level sales job is lightyears away from the dream job they truly desire.

So, I learned to switch the question.

If their answer to "What is your dream job?" is underwhelming, I follow up with an additional question:

"That's awesome. But, let me ask you this: if you had all of the resources, power, knowledge, and money in the world, what would your dream job be?"

Never has there been even one instance where the answer has not changed.

They'll respond with things like, "I wish I could photograph for **National Geographic**," or "I wish I could have an afternoon TV talk show," or "I wish I could travel the world playing music."

I always wonder what their lives would be like if they put their efforts towards achieving what they actually wanted.

"WOULD YOU STOP THINKING ABOUT WHAT EVERYONE WANTS? STOP THINKING ABOUT WHAT I WANT, WHAT HE WANTS, WHAT YOUR PARENTS WANT. WHAT DO YOU WANT? WHAT DO YOU WANT?"

Now, when you design your ideal, perfect routine, you should be as outrageous as you would like.

If your perfect morning routine includes someone waking you up by serenading you live with Beatles hits, write it down!

If you wish someone would bring you breakfast in bed, write it down!

If you wish you had a stylist to do your hair for you, or pick out your clothes, write it down!

If you wish you had a personal trainer to walk you through a consistent exercise program, write it down!

If you wish you had time to read in the morning, or if you wish you could have someone read to you, write it down!

If you wish you could have someone make your lunch in the morning, write it down!

47

Write down whatever you want!

This is your ideal routine.

So, begin to let your mind think about what your most perfect morning, evening, and eating routines would be.

We'll start crafting them in the next chapters.

WAX ON, WAX OFF.

Now, you might be saying to yourself, "I understand how someone could write a procedure for a more systematic process, like getting from Salt Lake City to Denver (like you talked about earlier). But, how does that relate to creating a routine?"

Just like you would write obnoxiously specific instructions for helping someone get from Salt Lake City to Denver, you will do the same for helping yourself get through your perfect morning routine.

I'VE GOT 99 PROBLEMS...AND THEY'RE SABOTAGING MY ROUTINES.

Have bad habits? Things you wish you could change?

Well, say "hello" to almost everyone else in the world.

But after you automate your routines, your problems will be eliminated!

When you design your perfect routine (step two), you will make sure that you have the problems (identified in step one) in mind.

Then, to combat these problems (i.e. bad habits) you will literally write activities, events, or people out of (or into) your routines and life.

IS THAT EVEN POSSIBLE?!

During this design portion (step two), you will treat your body as if it is a computer.

When you program a computer, you give obnoxiously specific instructions and directions.

For example:

- When someone pushes the bright blue button in the top, right-hand corner of the page, take them to Screen C.
- If they scroll down at least 1/3 of the page on Screen C., make Pop-Up A appear.
- If they don't click on Pop-Up A after 15 seconds, make Pop-Up B appear.
- Etc.

This level of specificity is exactly what we want to give to our bodies.

An example of a routine:

- Take earphones out from bathroom drawer
- Put into iPhone
- Start Spotify "Running" playlist
- Walk to front door
- Stretch right hamstring for fifteen seconds
- Stretch left hamstring for fifteen seconds
- Etc.

When you design a solution, you will create a step-by-step process for how you will achieve and follow the routine you want - your perfect routine.

GIVE IT TO ME STRAIGHT.

If you don't write your routines out step-by-step, I guarantee that you will fail. You will never, ever, be able to implement a routine that you want, let alone have it be automated.

Fun fact: the step-by-step part is where most people fall short.

In making goals, people too often say something like, "I'm going to earn $50,000 of additional income this year by doing affiliate marketing."

But, that's it! There is no process, no procedure, and no set of instructions that they've created to help them get there!

That is not what we will do here.

We're here to give you legitimate, actionable steps to give you legitimate, automated routines.

SUSHI MAKES ME VOMIT.

I think sushi tastes amazing. But, for whatever reason, I get queasy every time I eat it.

So, it's important that I know my capabilities.

No sashimi for me.

When coding, it's essential that you understand the capabilities of the computer you're programming.

So, as I'm sure you could guess, it's important that you understand your capabilities when designing your perfect routine.

Consider the following questions:

- Do I get overwhelmed easily?
- Am I a natural executer?
- Do I need people to be accountable to?
- Do I work better by myself?
- Do I work better with others?
- What do I do when I fall short?
- What do I naturally pay attention to?
- What comes easily for me?
- What do I struggle with?

Take the answers to these questions into consideration as you design your ideal morning, evening, and eating routines.

SORRY, THE CAVEMAN'S GOTCHA BEAT.

Do not reinvent the wheel.

If you are already good at something, great. Don't change that!

If you've been unsuccessful with a certain element of your routine in the past, don't implement the same strategy again!

For example, let's say you previously set a goal of eating healthy.

In an attempt to save you time and energy, you decided that you would prepare all of your food for the week on Sundays.

But, despite your intentions, you never actually followed through on this goal or plan.

Based on your past experiences, you would be foolish to try and set aside time on Sundays to prepare your meals again.

If it didn't work in the past, it probably won't work in the future! Think of something different!

Applying a proven, failed system is like putting orange juice into your car instead of fuel.

You know it isn't going to work.

But, for whatever reason, the orange juice is more easily accessible and easier to acquire than the fuel.

So, you put it in, hoping that the action of doing something will help.

But, the car is never going to run.

Never!

If you continue to apply "solutions" that have failed in the past, you are never going to achieve the results you desire.

3. CREATE YOUR PROGRAM

You've identified the problems that plague your routine (step one).

You've designed your perfect routine to eliminate those problems (step two).

And now, you're going to turn that perfect routine into a reality (step three)!

LET'S DO THIS THING.

Do you remember my brother who wanted to find one hundred new people to teach?

Once he created his "perfect" solution, he went back through and thought, "Could we make this happen?"

If they deemed a certain step of their routine absolutely impossible, they revised their program and substituted that step with the next best thing.

This allowed them to have the best, most effective, and realistic solution possible.

This is what we'll do here.

Step three of the formula, "creating your program," consists of three parts:

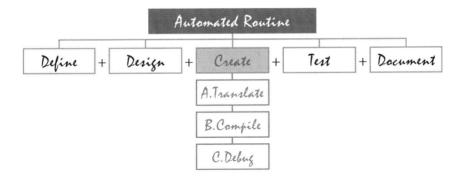

A. TRANSLATE YOUR PROGRAM

This is where you take your ideal routine and, through a series of questions and research, create a program that is as close to your ideal as possible.

B. COMPILE YOUR PROGRAM

Here's where the editing begins. You'll go back through and make sure that you haven't missed any holes in your routine.

C. DEBUGGING YOUR PROGRAM

When you debug, you declutter! You'll eliminate or store away anything that won't help you to achieve the routine automation success you desire.

Let's begin with the first part of creating your program.

A. TRANSLATE YOUR PROGRAM

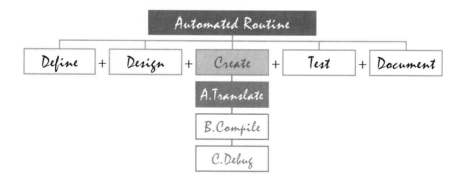

The only reason why you would translate something would be to make it easier to understand.

When coding, your objective is the same. You take your original designs (whether in plain English or flowchart form) and translate them into a programming language that is easier for a computer to understand.

The result might look something like this:

```
<!DOCTYPE html>
<html>
<body>
<h1>I am translating my instructions into a programming
language.</h1>
<p id="demo">Why?  Because my computer will understand it
better.</p>
<script>
function myFunction() {
    var x = document.getElementById("demo");
    x.style.fontSize = "25px";
    x.style.color = "red";
}</script>
<button type="button" onclick="myFunction()">Click Me!</button>
</body>
</html>
```

In routine automation, you take the perfect routine you designed and translate it into a series of steps that make it easier for you, the recipient of the information, to implement and follow.

As you do this, you will be shocked to see how many of these ideal elements of your routine can actually be accommodated.

For those things that you thought impossible, you may actually find many different ways to make them possible!

For example, if your ideal routine consisted of someone personally waking you up each morning while reciting motivational quotes from popular speeches, you could do a few things:

- Hire a virtual assistant to call you every morning
- Pre-record motivational quotes and have your alarm clock play them as the sound to wake you up
- After your alarm goes off, open an app that produces daily motivational quotes and read them out loud

You could even pay your mom or sibling to help you.

You might even consider exchanging a service with your spouse or a significant other.

There are so many ways to make what you want actually happen!

NO ONE CAN GO TO THE BATHROOM FOR YOU.

As you're translating your routine, there will be things that you can't delegate, modify, or eliminate.

The reasons for this may be due to expenses, or because they are just things that you really have to do yourself (shower, go to the restroom, etc.).

For these things, we'll talk later about how to automate them.

SNEAK PEEK INTO YOUR FUTURE.

To translate your designed solution, you'll go through each element of your drafted routine (whether a behavior, habit, or task) and ask yourself the following questions:

- Can I outsource this behavior?

If the answer is "no," you'll circle it. We'll learn how to automate these behaviors later.

If the answer is "yes," you'll continue through the following questions.

- Can I get someone to do this for me for free?
- Can I get an app to do it for free, or for a small cost?
- Can I afford to hire someone to do it for me?

By going through each of these questions, you will outsource as many possible behaviors and routines as possible, and then have the rest automated.

This means that you'll have a freakishly productive routine.

And, you'll have that freakishly productive morning routine consistently.

Tim Ferriss, a master of automation and outsourcing, said, "Never outsource something that can be eliminated, and never delegate something that can be streamlined. Otherwise, you waste somebody else's time instead of your own, which wastes your hard earned cash. Now how's that for an incentive to be effective and efficient?"

SHOW ME THE MONEY!

Here's a quick example of what this outsourcing process might look like:

In my personal evening routine, I wished that I would be asleep by 11:00pm every night. That way, when I woke up in the morning, I wouldn't feel like a truck had hit me the day before.

When designing my routine, I wanted someone to take away my computer at 10:00pm every night.

The internet was typically the reason for me staying up late, 'cause, you know...YouTube, Facebook, designing websites, etc.

But, if my computer were taken away at 10:00pm every night, this would allow me about thirty minutes to get ready for bed and at least thirty minutes to read at night before falling asleep at 11:00pm.

Sadly, I couldn't find anyone to consistently come over and take my computer away from me every day at 10pm.

So, I went through the questions and then asked myself, "Can I get an app to do it for free, or for a small cost?"

The answer? I wasn't sure.

I did some research and found an app called Freedom.

With it, you can shut off your internet (both on your computer and phone).

I created a schedule that shut my internet off at 10:00pm every day, and turned it back on again at 6:00am.

If it was really an emergency, I determined that I would use my roommate's computer.

This simple tweak in my routine has changed my whole life.

I've taken the decision away from myself to go to bed early (#fightdecisionfatigue).

I now go to bed by 11:00pm every night because all distractions (the internet) have been eliminated.

I have never felt more rested.

I have also never been more productive.

I hustle more throughout the day because I know I can't work at night.

I have also read twelve books in four weeks - more than I read all last year - because I made time for myself to read before bed.

I truly automated my behavior!

LAUNDRY IS FROM THE DEVIL.

Here's another example -

I HATE LAUNDRY.

It is the most time-consuming chore ever!

You have to separate your clothes, then put them in the wash, then wait, then switch them to the dryer, then wait, then fold your clothes, then put them away, and then hang up anything that needs to be hung up.

You then have to repeat the process, because who ever has only one load of laundry?

When designing my perfect routine, I wanted someone to completely take care of the whole laundry chore.

So, I went through the questions.

"Can I outsource it?"

The answer was yes!

I continued, "Can I get someone to do it for me for free?"

I am not married, nor was I dating someone at the time, nor was I in the same state as my mother.

So, I probably couldn't find someone to pawn this horrific chore off on.

I went to the next question, "Can I get an app to do it for free, or for a small cost?"

No. Unfortunately, an app couldn't do the trick.

I finally approached the last question: "Can I afford to hire someone to do it for me?"

I researched "laundry services in Utah" and found a company that would take my laundry and do it for $20/week.

All I had to do was put it out every Saturday, they would take it, and by the end of the day, it would be washed, folded, and back on my doorstep.

Problem solved. Routine simplified.

Now, my nemesis - laundry - is taken care of every week, automatically.

But, let's say that I didn't have $20 a week to spare on laundry.

I could search "I'm sick of doing my laundry," or "ways to get laundry done faster," or "how to make laundry easier" in Google.

I would come up with a slew of ways to make the whole laundry doing process less horrifically awful.

For example, you can do your laundry at a laundromat, so you can finish four loads at a time instead of one.

You also could schedule to do your laundry at the same time every week, so it doesn't interrupt other activities or responsibilities you have planned.

There are so many ways to solve and simplify certain tasks, or in our case, translate it to be more easily understood by the recipient of the program (aka you)!

As you research, you will find a lot of different solutions you can implement.

Remember, it is important to select whatever will most help you, your lifestyle, and the goals you're trying to accomplish.

B. COMPILE YOUR PROGRAM

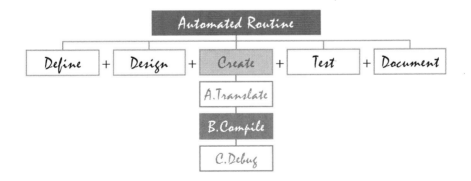

After we translate our designed solutions to make them easier for the recipient of the information (i.e. the computer, you) to understand, we compile what remains.

To compile something, it's as if we put it through a major editing process, making it even easier for the recipient of the information to understand.

When coders compile, they take the programming language they just created -

```
<!DOCTYPE html>
<html>
<body>
<h1>Yep, I'm still too hard for a computer to understand</h1>
<p>Compile me!</p>
<script>
window.alert(5 + 6);
</script>
</body>
</html>
```

- and transform it into something even easier (binary code aka 0's and 1's) for the computer to understand.

$$
\begin{pmatrix}
1 & 0 & 0 & 0 & 0 & 0 & 0 & 0 & 0 & 0 & 0 & 0 & 0 & 1 & 1 & 1 & 1 & 1 & 1 & 1 & 1 & 1 \\
0 & 1 & 0 & 0 & 0 & 0 & 0 & 0 & 0 & 0 & 0 & 0 & 1 & 1 & 1 & 0 & 1 & 1 & 1 & 0 & 0 & 0 & 1 \\
0 & 0 & 1 & 0 & 0 & 0 & 0 & 0 & 0 & 0 & 0 & 0 & 1 & 1 & 0 & 1 & 1 & 1 & 0 & 0 & 0 & 1 & 0 \\
0 & 0 & 0 & 1 & 0 & 0 & 0 & 0 & 0 & 0 & 0 & 0 & 1 & 0 & 1 & 1 & 1 & 0 & 0 & 0 & 1 & 0 & 1 \\
0 & 0 & 0 & 0 & 1 & 0 & 0 & 0 & 0 & 0 & 0 & 0 & 1 & 1 & 1 & 1 & 0 & 0 & 0 & 1 & 0 & 1 & 1 \\
0 & 0 & 0 & 0 & 0 & 1 & 0 & 0 & 0 & 0 & 0 & 0 & 1 & 1 & 1 & 0 & 0 & 0 & 1 & 0 & 1 & 1 & 0 \\
0 & 0 & 0 & 0 & 0 & 0 & 1 & 0 & 0 & 0 & 0 & 0 & 1 & 1 & 0 & 0 & 0 & 1 & 0 & 1 & 1 & 0 & 1 \\
0 & 0 & 0 & 0 & 0 & 0 & 0 & 1 & 0 & 0 & 0 & 0 & 1 & 0 & 0 & 0 & 1 & 0 & 1 & 1 & 0 & 1 & 1 \\
0 & 0 & 0 & 0 & 0 & 0 & 0 & 0 & 1 & 0 & 0 & 0 & 1 & 0 & 0 & 1 & 0 & 1 & 1 & 0 & 1 & 1 & 1 \\
0 & 0 & 0 & 0 & 0 & 0 & 0 & 0 & 0 & 1 & 0 & 0 & 1 & 0 & 1 & 0 & 1 & 1 & 0 & 1 & 1 & 1 & 0 \\
0 & 0 & 0 & 0 & 0 & 0 & 0 & 0 & 0 & 0 & 1 & 0 & 1 & 1 & 0 & 1 & 1 & 0 & 1 & 1 & 1 & 0 & 0 \\
0 & 0 & 0 & 0 & 0 & 0 & 0 & 0 & 0 & 0 & 0 & 1 & 1 & 0 & 1 & 1 & 0 & 1 & 1 & 1 & 0 & 0 & 0 \\
\end{pmatrix}
$$

Interestingly, computers don't actually understand some programming languages.

60

They really only understand binary code, something that is made up of 0's and 1's.

Thus, compiling is essential.

COME WITH YOUR "A" GAME.

If any part of the code is written incorrectly when it is input into a compiling service (what will turn it to 0's and 1's), the system will complain.

Compiling services are extremely particular about syntax rules. If you are missing a comma, or if you spell something incorrectly within the programming language, it will let you know.

BE OBNOXIOUSLY THOROUGH.

Your routines must go through the same amount of scrutiny!

Things must be as exact and thorough as possible.

If they aren't, your entire routines will be derailed!

Here's what that might look like:

You've just finished showering. You temporarily leave the bathroom to go get your clothes. But, as you're gone, your roommate/husband/child enters the bathroom.

You never accounted for this happening.

Because this was not a part of your routine (or, because you didn't think to bring your clothes into the bathroom with you so you never had to leave), your routine has been derailed (the figurative compiling system would complain)!

"What's the big deal?"

When our routines are interrupted, we typically revert back to our old habits like watching Netflix, going on Facebook, or doing something that doesn't adhere to our end goals.

So, the more thorough you are with your routines, the better.

CROSS YOUR "T'S" AND DOT YOUR "I'S."

A compiled routine can be identified by its specificity.

For example, a routine would never pass the compiling stage if it was presented like this:

- Wake up
- Exercise

Instead, a routine should look like this:

- Alarm goes off at 6:30am
- Consciously choose to open eyes
- Unplug phone from charger
- Take phone, while the alarm is still ringing, out of room
- Take phone into the bathroom
- Turn off the alarm when inside the bathroom
- Change into workout clothes (that were placed in the bathroom the night before)
- Grab headphones from drawer
- Breathe deeply for forty breaths
- Start music playlist
- Leave bathroom
- Immediately exit through front door
- Start running pre-determined route
- Etc.

Which routine is more likely to happen?

The second!

And, as you do the steps outlined in the second routine over and over again, they will become automated - second nature. They will require no more conscious thought.

If you stick with the "Wake up, exercise" plan, the compiler system will be furious!

Why? Because the routine is ambiguous. There is too much room for error and too many opportunities for old habits to infiltrate your new, ideal routine.

So, in the compiling portion of the formula, we will go back through our translated routines and flesh them out anywhere instruction is unclear or non-existent.

Leave no room for error.

C. DEBUG YOUR PROGRAM

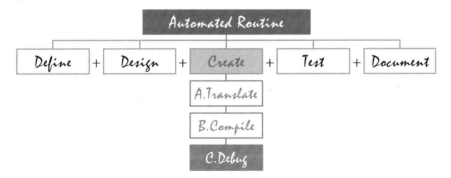

In the world of routine automation, "debugging" is interchangeable with "decluttering."

Even though this portion of the formula is simply a sub-step, its execution, in my opinion, results most directly to the success of automated routines.

"I'M SORRY, WHAT DID YOU JUST SAY?"

Oh, you want me to repeat that insanely important sentence above? Sure, I'd be happy to.

Even though this portion of the formula is simply a sub-step, its execution, in my opinion, results most directly to the success of automated routines.

After you've translated and compiled your program, it's time to eliminate anything that could prohibit or distract you from obtaining your routine automation goals.

Here is where we combat decision fatigue.

Let me explain:

Meet Jeff. Hi, Jeff. We like your beard, Jeff (and so does Ke$ha).

Jeff has set a goal to eat healthier.

So, he goes through the formula: defines the problem, designs his ideal solution, and has now translated and compiled it.

As part of his program, he decides to eat the same breakfast every morning - steel cut oats.

If Jeff didn't declutter, he would go buy the oats, and simply add them to his pantry.

Note that his pantry is already filled with food that he has purchased previously (pasta, macaroni and cheese, Ramen, tortillas, peanut butter, bagels, etc.).

The next morning, Jeff goes to his pantry and sees his steel oats.

He contemplates the decision to take the time to make them.

But, he is tempted by the bagel that is sitting right next to his steel cut oats.

He could also eat the Eggo waffles in his freezer or the high-fat yogurt in his fridge.

If you disregard human reason and personal preference, Jeff has a one in four chance of actually eating the steel cut oats over the bagel, Eggos, or yogurt (that's 25% for all you Mathletes out there).

If you account for human reason and personal preference, Jeff could have more than a 25% chance of eating the steel cut oats. But, that percentage will change every day, depending on how steel-cut-oat-y Jeff feels.

But, if Jeff had debugged his program (aka decluttered), he would have discarded or given away any food that didn't directly contribute to him fulfilling his goal of eating healthier.

More specifically, he would have discarded any breakfast food that was not steel cut oats.

That way, when he wakes up in the morning, he has exactly one choice of what to eat for breakfast: steel cut oats.

And, because he only has one choice of what to eat for breakfast, he will choose it, every time - increasing his odds from a varying 25% success rate to a definite, automatic 100%.

Declutter, declutter, declutter, declutter!

JUST MAKE IT EASY FOR YOURSELF, WON'TCHA?

If you have too many choices pulling you away from your routine, you will struggle.

If you are frantically looking for items that will help you fulfill your routines, you will also struggle.

For example, if part of your routine is to floss every day, but you have no idea where your floss is, then you probably are not going to floss.

Finally, if you know where the items are that you need to fulfill your routines, but they're not in the location where you typically fulfill your routines, you will fail.

For example, if you want to take your multivitamin every night before you go to bed and your vitamins are downstairs in the kitchen, but you get ready for bed in your master bathroom, then you're probably not going to be taking your multivitamin every day.

All of these issues could be eliminated by decluttering!

TEACH ME, SENSEI.

To effectively debug or declutter, identify all of the locations where you will be implementing your routine.

Within those locations, identify different areas where you feel cluttered.

For example, I fulfill my morning routine in my:

- Bedroom
- Bathroom
- Living room
- Kitchen

When I set out to debug these areas, here is where I felt cluttered:

- **Bedroom**
    - Closet
    - Clothes drawers
    - Desk drawers
    - Bookshelf
    - Underneath my bed
- **Bathroom**
    - Underneath sink
    - Bathroom drawer
    - Make-up bag
- **Living room**
    - Bookshelf
    - TV cabinet
- **Kitchen**
    - Pantry
    - Fridge
    - Freezer

After you've done this, go through and ruthlessly eliminate anything that isn't going to help you fulfill your routines.

"BUT, WHAT IF I PLAN ON BEING A CREEPY CAT LADY WHO HOARDS EVERYTHING?"

If you plan on being a creepy cat lady who hoards everything, then I'm seriously confused about how you've made it this far into the book.

Either way, it can be hard to let go of things, because shoot - we just get too sentimental, sometimes.

Going through these questions as you declutter will help you determine what to do:

- Will this help me fulfill my routine?

If "yes," then ask:

- Is there anything I could do to make it more easily accessible to make my routine run more smoothly?

If "no," then ask:

- Can I eliminate it/throw it away?

If "no," then ask:

- Can I store it?

If "no," then ask:

- Can I arrange it so it doesn't interfere with my routine?

I guarantee that the answer to at least one of those questions will be "yes!"

TOUGH LOVE, FROM ME TO YOU.

Don't allow your routine automation to be hindered because you were too lazy to discard things that weren't necessary.

In *Deep Work* by Cal Newport, he tells the story of a man who, in an attempt to declutter his life and increase his productivity, packed up every item of his apartment.

For the next three weeks, he only took things out of boxes as he needed them.

Time passed and he realized that he had hardly taken out anything.

So, after the three weeks, he gathered all of the items that he had yet to unpack, and donated them.

This is an extreme example, but it shows the power that simplicity can have on increased productivity, or, in our case, routine automation.

Just to get some ideas going in your head, here are some places where I needed to declutter while creating my routines:

- **Room and drawers in my closet**
  - Ended up donating two bags of clothes to Goodwill.

- **Freezer**
  - Finally threw away the pineapple flavored bratwursts that my mom lovingly bought me from Costco. It was kind of her, but wow, they sounded so disgusting I could never bring myself to eat them.

- **Fridge**
  - I share an apartment with my roommates. And, they love me more now because my eating routine only takes up 1/6 of the fridge. You're welcome for the extra space.

- **Car**
  - My car was embarrassingly messy. But, she is clean now. Also, she is a white Toyota Rav4 named Squanto. So, wave and say "hello" if you see her.

- **Evernote**
  - This note-taking program on my computer was chalk full of chaotically organized goodness. So, I eliminated, consolidated, and archived. My self-diagnosed OCD has never been more satisfied.

- **Facebook**
  - I deleted the app off my phone. It wasn't adhering to my goals. I also implemented the Facebook Eradicator Chrome Extension, which blocks my news feed. Now, I can still use Facebook, but I'm not bombarded with everyone's news. It's awesome.

- **Pocket**

    - Another Chrome Extension that lets you tag articles you'd like to read later. Long story short, I had collected too many articles. So, just as I did with Evernote, I eliminated, consolidated, and archived.

- **Email**

    - I had too many labels. So, I simplified. Inbox zero is now the norm rather than the one-time highlight of my year.

        - P.S. I use tools like Boomerang and Unroll.me, along with Google Filters, to make inbox zero a consistent reality.

- **Instagram**

    - I unfollowed anyone that was distracting, demeaning, or disgusting (aka crude). I also turned off my notifications.

- **YouTube**

    - Unsubscribed from all the crazies. And yep - notifications were turned off.

I have more examples of places that I've decluttered, but I simply wanted to give you ideas of locations that could be debugged. Once again, don't worry! In the following chapters, I will walk you through how you can execute this entire process for your routines.

ORIENT ME AGAIN, PLEASE?

At this point, you will have completed each of the three parts (translating, compiling, and debugging) of the third step in the formula, "create your program."

4. TEST THE PROGRAM

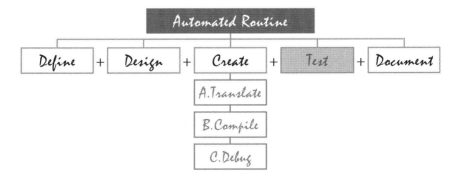

In the fourth step of the formula, "test the program," you will actually implement your newly crafted routine!

By this point, you will have a whole routine written out.

Your routine includes actionable steps that have been translated, compiled, and debugged to ensure that it will run smoothly, and actually work.

PATIENCE YOU MUST HAVE, MY YOUNG PADAWAN.

Thanks, Yoda.

Now, how you go about implementing your routine is extremely important.

When you begin the implementation of your routine, it is essential that you follow each step in its exact order.

- Do not skip steps.
- Do not reorder the steps.
- If, for whatever reason, you skip a step, you must start your routine over.

It is very important that you follow the process exactly.

RE-READ YODA'S COMMENT ABOVE.

Remember, you are programming your body!

By doing things in the same way, and in the same order, every day, the routine will become automatic. Your body will start to take control.

Things that used to be excruciating will now be handled on autopilot!

Practicing your ideal routines over and over again will permit behaviors to become second nature.

Very quickly, you will start preserving your brainpower, saving your time, and creating consistency in your life.

Your routines will no longer require "conscious thought," and will thus become automatic.

A STORY ABOUT THE ACTUAL PIANO GUY IN THE BAND, THE PIANO GUYS.

His name is Jon Schmidt.

He's an exceptional musician, an amazing performer, and he writes music that is seriously fun to play.

He also devised an extremely effective way to teach new students the piano.

The basis of his method centers around what he calls the "Blow Up Game."

When playing the "Blow Up Game," a brand new piano student is given a line of music.

They are instructed to play each note exactly as it is played.

The catch?

Schmidt explains to the student, "Very important: Tell your brain it needs to be careful to get it right on the first try. Pretend you will blow up if you miss...take your time...touch the note...double check...play. (Repeat as needed.)"

He continues,

> Training the brain to expect to get it right the first time is of utmost importance! This means that it will be painfully slow. Allow 10 to 20 seconds per note column, possibly longer if there are two notes in a column. Try to at least get to the point where they have successfully read an entire line with no "blow ups". Tell the student: "take your time...touch the note...double check...play.

At the end of this portion of his teaching, he answers a common question, "Should we care how bad the songs sound?"

He replies,

> It is not going to sound anything like the real song. It is simply a process of becoming familiar with how note reading works. At the seven week mark you will start focusing on making things sound good, but until then, the playing you hear will be painfully slow and will not resemble music at all. It will require a certain amount of patience. The good news is that it is surprising how much the beginner enjoys it.

Though the start is tedious, students who implement Schmidt's piano learning methodology can play advanced music in only a matter of weeks.

This same system of going through each action step by step, and allowing no "blow ups" in the implementation of routines, is what will allow your routines to become automated.

HOW AM I SUPPOSED TO REMEMBER MY FIFTY STEP ROUTINE WHEN I CAN'T EVEN REMEMBER MY OWN PHONE NUMBER?

To help with the implementation of my ideal routines, I use an iPhone application called "Productive."

It was $3.99, and worth every cent.

The app allows you to input every ounce of your routine.

When you complete a task, you can swipe right, a happy little "ding" will sound, and the task disappears.

Here is how a series of tasks within my evening routines looks:

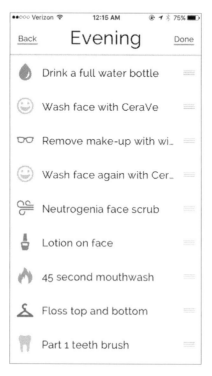

When I began trying to automate this routine, I would follow it in the exact order that I wrote it.

If I missed a step, I would start over.

I was frustrated at first, but I knew that if I didn't do these behaviors in the same order, my routine would never become completely automatic (which was the result I wanted).

Interestingly, after four days, I didn't need to use the app anymore.

My routine had become second nature.

Not just one habit. Or two. Or even three.

My entire routine, comprising over fifty actions, became completely automated in four days.

How's that for amazing?

Sure, it took a little bit of time up front, but I was able to automate a routine that I had struggled with for the past twenty-four years of my life.

The initial work of going through the programming process, and then testing and implementing my routine in this way was all worth it.

I finally had the set, consistent, and ideal routines that I had always wanted!

"BUT, DOESN'T IT GET BORING DOING THE SAME THINGS ALL THE TIME?"

Can I counter that with, "Well, you were going to have to shower every day for the rest of your life anyway. Now, it's just faster, easier, and automatic."

It really is amazing.

Your body will start to love you for implementing these routines.

Your body will start to crave food at certain times.

And, it will start to crave the food you want it to crave.

You won't be tired when you wake up.

And, you'll start to feel tired at your designated bedtime.

Our bodies are completely programmable. We just have to be smart about how we do it.

DIDN'T SEE THAT ONE COMIN'.

It's important to note that even the most experienced programmers have errors in their code (even after they compile and debug it).

So, don't be discouraged if you encounter stumbling blocks in your routine!

Why?

When you compile and debug a program, you can ensure that it is written correctly.

But, you cannot ensure that it is solving the original problem.

This can be compared to a sentence that is syntactically correct, but semantically incorrect.

For example, take the sentence, "Colorless green ideas sleep furiously."

Grammatically, that sentence is correct.

But, semantically? I have absolutely no idea what the heck that sentence is trying to communicate.

Thus, testing is necessary.

And some modifications will be necessary.

"DON'T GO CHANGIN', TO TRY AND--"...ACTUALLY, SCRATCH THAT; CHANGE IS GOOD.

Modifications are actually great things!

As you get smarter and better at implementing your routines, you'll find places where you can intensify your routine, or change it to adhere more precisely to the goals you want to accomplish.

As you go through your routines, it is important that you continually ask yourself these questions:

- How can I modify my routine to make it easier to automate?
- What am I falling short on?
- Is it really important?
- If it's not really important, can I eliminate it?
- Is it too hard? How can I simplify it?
- Is it being sabotaged by another habit (whether good or bad)?

As an example, I set the goal (like every other human in this world) to start working out.

I first began by trying to go to CrossFit every day.

Going from no exercise to CrossFit (an extremely intense form of exercise) was not my smartest idea.

I'm actually kind of embarrassed.

After paying for three months (at $100/month) and going less than ten days, I realized that it was more important for me to develop the habit of moving my body every day (rather than completing the actual CrossFit program).

(To all you CrossFitters out there, you are an inspiration.)

So, I modified my routine.

I thought, "What would be an exercise that I could do that I would feel confident that I could complete every day?"

I now go on a one mile run every day.

And it's the same one mile run every day.

And I listen to the same playlist every day.

But, because my objective was to develop a habit of exercising, rather than focus on the exercise itself, it is considered a success.

As my exercise goals change, my routine will need to be modified again.

And that is more than okay.

Here is a powerful quote from Bill Gates, founder of Microsoft. He said, "The first rule of any technology used in a business is that automation applied to an efficient operation will magnify the efficiency. The second is that any automation applied to an inefficient operation will magnify the inefficiency."

Test your program, implement it properly, and modify as needed.

5. DOCUMENT YOUR PROGRAM

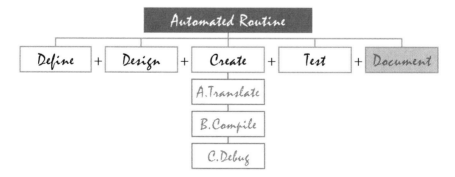

The final step of this process is documentation.

You absolutely have to write down the program you create!

In coding, the documentation of a program includes the following:

- The original nature of the problem
- A brief description of the design
- The program itself
- The tested results and modifications

Why do I recommend that you complete this step to finalize your routine automation?

Because it will supplement your human memory.

Humans are prone to forget.

Documentation provides evidence of your experimental results and allows you to mark your progress.

And, as you improve in your ability to automate your routines (or, as your financial situation or relationship status changes) you will be able to incorporate more aspects of your original, ideal plan that you developed in step two, "design a solution."

I'll show you examples of how to do this (and more about why to do this) when we create your morning routine.

I AGREE WITH K.G. - ANYTHING IS POSSIBLE!

To summarize, here is the process required to create a routine that you can then automate:

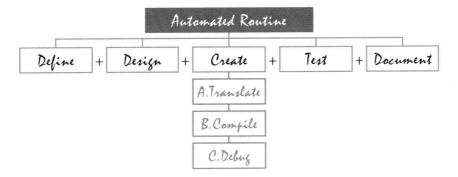

1. Define the problem
2. Design a solution
3. Create your program
4. Test your program
5. Document your program

Follow this formula and

- Your routines will be perfectly constructed
- They'll contain specific processes and procedures of how to complete them
- And they'll be completely debugged and easy to implement

This means that your routines, and your results, will become automated.

PUT ME IN, COACH!

It's time for you to create these routines for yourself!

We'll make sure that we do everything necessary to automate the elements of your routines that are stressful, boring, and difficult.

You will experience an increase in willpower, a more keen ability to think and problem solve, a greater consistency in life, and the automatic results that accompany routines.

Shall we get started?

The first essential step is next!

CHAPTER 5:

YOUR "WHY" WILL GOVERN YOUR "TRY"

I know I just made it sound like we were going to go through the five-step formula to start creating your routines, but we're not (yet).

I'm sorry.

But, actually, I'm not sorry at all.

I SIT, AND WONDER WHY-YI-YI, OH WHY?

Before creating any routine, you must understand the "why" behind your efforts.

- Why do you want to automate your routines?
- Why do you want to be consistent?
- Why do you want to eliminate stressful, boring, and difficult things from your life?

You might also consider -

- What will it do for you?
- Who will it help you to become?
- What are you trying to accomplish?

If there is no reason behind your automating efforts, all you'll be left with is, "Yay! I automated my morning routine and now I have time to focus on nothing because I didn't think this far ahead!"

Eventually, your automating will fall apart because you'll simply be doing actions for the sake of doing actions.

If you were a computer, that wouldn't matter.

But - news flash - you're a human.

gasp

We can apply a lot of principles from programming computers to programming humans.

But, at the end of the day, regardless of whether you have red hair or not, you have a soul.

So, having meaning and purpose behind activities contributes markedly to the success of your actions.

Before we get into the five-step formula to program your body and automate your morning, evening, and eating routines, let's ensure that you understand the reasoning behind why you want to automate anything in the first place.

It will be one of the most important differences in making your desired automated routines a reality.

A TWO-MONTH PATERNAL LEAVE.

Remember Mark Zuckerberg, the founder of Facebook that we talked about earlier?

He and his wife had a baby on December 1, 2015.

He recently said that after having had his baby, he wanted to make sure that "his days counted."

This is probably why he went on a two-month paternity leave once his child was born, something that is almost completely unheard of amongst professionals in Silicon Valley.

But, after the two months, it was time for him to go back to work.

On that day, he posted a picture to social media that said, "First day back to work. What should I wear?"

The picture that he included showed off his extremely diverse clothing selection. LOL.

Jokingly, he poked fun at his simple, consistent, and automatic wardrobe.

But, it's clear that the time he spent with his wife and new baby was enhanced because he wasn't bogged down or distracted by unnecessary or mundane decisions or tasks like choosing what to wear.

He automated his routines so that his "days counted."

WHAT'S YOUR REASON?

Let's say I posed the question, "Why are you choosing to automate your behaviors?"

You could say, "Oh, it's to eliminate stress," or "I want to free up my time."

Okay, but...so what?

You want to eliminate your stress so you can become who?

Or, you want to free up your time so you can accomplish what?

Imagine if waking up in the morning was simple.

Imagine if you didn't dread preparing meals every day.

Imagine if you actually went to bed with a clear mind.

What would happen to the middle of your day if the beginning and ending were executed flawlessly?

Take time to answer these questions.

These are the two questions you need to answer:

1.   Who do you want to become by automating your routines?

2.   What do you want to accomplish by automating your routines?

The answers to these questions will serve as your end goals.

They will help you to shape your routines.

Answer these questions by creating written principles for yourself.

Principles are more guidelines, or foundational truths, rather than specifics.

I know, I know, it goes against everything I just said in the last chapter about being insanely and obnoxiously specific.

But, for the "why," I want you to answer with a principle, because principles help you to shape decisions in your life.

Some great principle answers to "Who do you want to become?" might include:

- I want to become patient.
- I want to become tolerant.
- I want to become consistent.

- I want to become forthcoming.

- I want to become intentional.

You could then use those principles to shape exactly what you want your morning, evening, and eating routines to look like.

Someone that is seeking to become patient might have a different routine than someone who is seeking to become forthcoming.

For example, someone seeking patience might meditate first thing in the morning so they can start their day in a calm, centered manner, while someone striving to become more forthcoming might participate in a high-intensity group spin class right after they wake up so they're ready to attack their day head on.

KNOW THYSELF.

I recently joined an online course called *Self-Publishing School.*

This course teaches you how to become a successful Kindle author.

Before we ever start writing or even learn how to write, the creator of the course invites us to go through an exercise where we determine why we want to write a book.

My initial thought was, "I want to write a book because I want to create a solid source of passive income that will fuel my financial success."

But, as I pondered this more, I thought, "If I were completely financially successful, and would be for the rest of my life, would I be satisfied?"

I realized that the answer was, "No."

I had to go back and re-evaluate the reason why I wanted to write a book.

As I thought about it more, I realized that I didn't desire money. Rather, I craved the freedom to learn whatever I wanted to learn, whenever I wanted to learn it, from whoever I wanted to learn from.

My thought changed: "Writing a solid series of books will provide me with opportunities to become an expert in a field, which will allow me to connect with other experts in the habit formation and routine automating world. I will also be able to earn money so that I can take courses, classes, and hire people to teach me different skills. It will allow me to travel to meet people. By earning more money, it would also free up my time to be able to learn the things I want to learn."

When I really understood the reason behind why I wanted to write books, it shaped my actions.

I became happy to make sacrifices to accomplish my work because I understood what I was working toward.

So, before you go through the effort that will be required to automate your routines, I want to invite you to answer the question, "Why?"

Why do you want to automate your routines?

More specifically,

- Who do you want to become because of your routine automation?
- What do you want to accomplish because of your routine automation?

Once you have these answers, flip the page and we'll start automating your morning routine.

CHAPTER 6:

AUTOMATE YOUR MORNING ROUTINE

*If you're wanting to get started right away (or you're revisiting this chapter), make sure to download the **Automate Your Routines, Guarantee Your Results Workbook.***

Can I get an "amen"?!

Typically, morning routines are the hardest for people to conquer.

But, in this chapter, we're going to change that. Prepare yourself to create your own automated morning routine!

WHY IT'S WORTH IT.

After you automate your morning routine, here are some benefits that you'll experience:

- **Bring it on (in a non-cheerleader kind of way)**

Remember the whole "don't check your email right when you wake up" example that we went through earlier?

By starting your day in a proactive state, rather than a reactive state, you will consciously be taking action toward the life you want.

You will be more focused.

Also, your efforts will be consistent, not sporadic, which means that you'll see consistent results.

- **You'll be the Henry Ford of productivity**

Remember when Henry Ford introduced assembly lines into the world and insanely increased his company's productivity level?

That's what will happen to you.

Studies have shown that a person's most productive hours are two to three hours after they first wake up.

If you follow a morning routine, you'll prepare to meet your body and mind at their peak of productivity each day.

- **Bump, set, spike**

When you automate your morning routine, you set the tone of your day!

We've all had that feeling of looking at our clock, realizing we've slept through our alarm, and knowing that there is absolutely no way we're going to be able to pull off getting to work on time.

The only benefit to that is that your heart races so fast that it compensates for not working out that day.

Regardless, it's the worst.

By automating your morning routine, you'll never have to feel that way again!

Because you have already accomplished all you need to in the morning, you free up your afternoons and evenings.

Really, it just feels nice to be taking over the world when most people haven't even thought about waking up.

An automated routine also means no more "Oh, you look tired" comments from socially unaware people.

Now, let's start automating your morning routine. Here we go!

1. DEFINE THE PROBLEM

Suggested time to complete: 10 minutes total

Whether your current morning routine is extremely defined or completely non-existent, I want you to start walking through what a typical morning looks like for you.

As you focus on your routine, answer the following questions:

- **What is boring about your morning routine?**

Example: I hate blow drying my hair. It's so loud that I can't listen to music or an audiobook while I do it.

- **What is stressful about your morning routine?**

Example: I never wake up with enough time to get ready, so I'm always hustling to get out the door.

- **What is difficult about your morning routine?**

Example: Eating in the morning is literally difficult for me. My body seems to reject all food before 11:00am. I feel like throwing up whenever I even think about eating in the morning.

89

YOU'RE NOT ALONE.

If you're not quite sure what problems plague your morning routine, here are some common complaints to get your ideas flowing:

- "I need at least three alarms to get me up in the morning."
- "Even after I wake up, I need at least fifteen minutes before I can get my brain to focus on anything."
- "I fall asleep in the shower. Every day."
- "I fall asleep on the toilet. Every day."
- "Working out in the morning? You're kidding, right?"
- "I go to work every day with a wrinkly shirt. Who has time to iron?!"
- "Doing my hair and makeup at an early hour result in me looking crazy - we're talking Lady Gaga style. I just can't focus!"
- "I never eat breakfast because I never have time."

ISN'T COMPLAINING BAD?

As you start to understand the problems that have infiltrated your morning routine, you will start to understand just how dysfunctional your mornings have been.

But, don't be discouraged! This newfound knowledge will help you realize how desperately you need to automate your routines.

These defined problems will help shape the design of your ideal routine (step two).

But, before then, complete the action steps below.

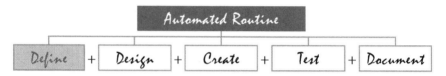

(COMPLETE ALL ACTION STEPS IN YOUR *Automate Your Routines, Guarantee Your Results WORKBOOK!*)

ACTION STEPS

Suggested time to complete: 10 minutes

> *"I celebrate myself, and sing myself"*
> *(Walt Whitman, Leaves of Grass)*

Give at least three answers to the following questions:

1. What is boring about my morning routine?
2. What is stressful about my morning routine?
3. What is difficult about my morning routine?

PITFALLS TO AVOID

- Do not discard any problem because it seems too trivial or too monumental.

As long as what you write down answers the three questions above, you're golden!

WHEN YOUR THUNDER THIGHS FAIL YOU.

For example, one of my answers to "What is difficult about your morning routine?" was "I get tired standing up the whole time while getting ready."

Some might think that's pathetic.

Me, on the other hand, think, "My thunder thighs weren't made for this. Get me a chair."

HELPFUL TOOLS:

- *Automate Your Routines, Guarantee Your Results Workbook*

2. DESIGN A SOLUTION

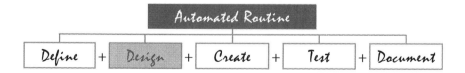

WHO RUNS THE WORLD?

It's time to design your ideal routine!

While looking at the problems you identified in step one, think, "If I could create the perfect routine that would eliminate all of these problems, what would it look like?"

Be as specific and as ridiculous as possible. Like we discussed before - if your ideal routine includes having someone read to you in a British accent in the morning, then write it down!

As a side note, at this point in the formula, do not worry about allocating time to your desired activities. Thoughts like, "Oh, this could never happen because I only have one hour in the morning" should be thrown aside.

Remember, at this stage of the formula, you are thinking as if your resources (including time) are unlimited.

Do not put any restraints on your mind or creativity as you design this routine.

While completing this, I recommend a twenty minute brain dump with a twenty-five minute revision period.

HERE'S WHAT I MEAN BY THAT.

To start designing your ideal routine, put a timer on your phone for twenty minutes. Turn off your internet, turn your phone to airplane mode, and do not allow anything to distract you.

Then, start your timer and write down everything that you wish was in your morning routine.

Everything!

If you believe that you've thought of everything, but you've only been brainstorming for twelve minutes, keep going! It's when we push ourselves and really exercise our brain as a muscle that better, more refined, and more authentic ideas arise.

So, don't stop early!

I recommend doing this on a piece of paper. But, if you're set on typing it out, I really love the app WriteRoom.

It blocks out your entire screen, so all you can see is the writing page. It is excellent for helping you to stay focused.

```
This is what the app WriteRoom looks like.

It blocks everything out while you type, leaving you to create the most epic
morning routine ever.

*HIGH FIVE*
```

Whatever tool you choose to use, brain dump for twenty minutes!

"I'M AFRAID TO SEE WHAT'S IN MY MIND."

Don't worry, I was too.

Here are some examples of ideas that came from my brain dump:

- I want someone to come cook me a healthy breakfast every morning.
- I want a personal trainer to come to my house, get me out of bed, and force me to work out with him in the morning.
- I want to wake up and never be tired.
- I want to wake up and feel excited about my life.
- I want to have a stylist come and do my hair and makeup for me each day.
- I want to have time to read in the morning.
- I want to never feel rushed in the morning.

Get the idea? Brain dump!

YOU'VE BEEN DUMPED (IT'S NOT YOU, IT'S ME).

After you brain dump, set a new timer on your phone for twenty-five minutes.

During these twenty-five minutes, you're going to take all of the ideas that you wrote down and start creating a chronological order of your routine.

Based on my brain dump above, I could say something like:

1. Have someone personally wake me up when I am in the lightest level of sleep so waking up is as painless as possible.

2. To make sure I am excited for the day, have someone ask me, right as I get out of bed, how I am going to make the day worthwhile.

3. Immediately change into my workout clothes that I have set out the night before.

4. Meet my personal trainer at my front door.

5. Go with him to the gym.

6. Etc.

Get the picture? Start to draft your perfect morning routine.

Remember, the more specific the steps, the better.

If you have more than two hundred action items in your morning routine, great! Remember, you are creating your ideal routine, so length and time do not matter.

As a side note, I would recommend not doing any research online at this point. Right now, you want to cultivate your genuine desires. The more time you allow for your own ideas to surface, the more satisfying your ultimate routine will be.

DID YOU FORGET SOMETHING?

As you go through your twenty minute brain dump and your twenty-five minute revision, consider these elements that typically comprise morning routines:

- Wake up
- Connect with a higher power
- Exercise
- Breakfast
- Shower/get ready
- Read/consume beneficial content
- Learn a new skill
- Plan for the day

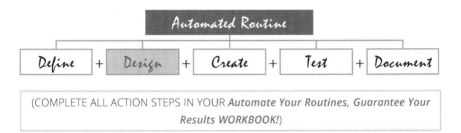

(COMPLETE ALL ACTION STEPS IN YOUR *Automate Your Routines, Guarantee Your Results WORKBOOK!*)

ACTION STEPS

Suggested time to complete: 45 minutes total

> *"We have all a better guide in ourselves, if we would attend to it, than any other person can be."*
> (Jane Austen, Mansfield Park)

Complete the following two tasks:

- Eliminate all distractions and do a twenty minute brain dump, answering the question, "What would my ideal morning routine look like?"

Remember, for this exercise, think as if you have all of the time, money, and resources in the world!

- With distractions still eliminated, take twenty-five minutes to revise your brain dump and organize your brainstormings into a chronological order.

Fill in any holes and flesh out any ideas. The goal is to have a complete, perfect routine by the end of the twenty-five minutes.

PITFALLS TO AVOID

- Don't worry about feeling selfish or guilty for wanting the routine you want. If you wish someone would fan you with giant palm tree leaves after you come home from a morning run, then by all means, write it down.

- Don't justify your ideas away! "Oh, this could never work," or "this will never happen" are the worst things that could possibly be going through your head.

This is an exercise. Don't suppress or extinguish any thoughts!

- Don't feel discouraged.

As you're making your ideal routine, you may realize just how different your current routine is from your ideal routine.

But, do not become discouraged!

Instead, realize that by defining your ideal, you're one step closer to actually achieving it.

You now have something to work towards.

HELPFUL TOOLS:

- *Automate Your Routines, Guarantee Your Results Workbook*
- *Pen and paper*
- *WriteRoom app* (blocks out the whole screen as you write)
- *Freedom app* (blocks out the internet for however long you'd like)
- *Timer+ app* (my favorite timer tool)

Optional tools

- If you're struggling (and I mean really struggling) to generate your ideal morning routine, check out these people's morning routines to spark some ideas.

  - *MyMorningRoutine.com*

  - *7 Morning Routines for Business and Personal Success* (link in Workbook)

3. CREATE YOUR PROGRAM

Suggested time to complete: 4 hours total

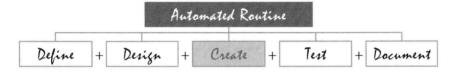

MY DREAM CAR IS A VOLKSWAGON VAN.

To illustrate what creating your program looks like, consider this example:

You've just spent time designing the perfect blueprint to make your ideal car (i.e. designing your ideal routine).

Now, you're going to take those blueprints and manufacture them to become an actual functioning, working vehicle (i.e. creating your program).

Remember that creating your program consists of three parts: translating your solution, compiling your program, and debugging your program.

Let's get ready to rumble.

A. TRANSLATE YOUR SOLUTION

Suggested time to complete: 1.5 hours total

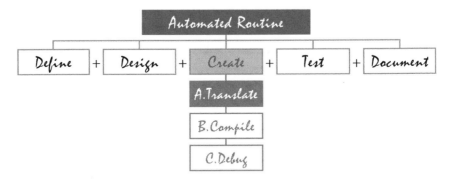

With your design in hand, take each item of your routine and filter it through the following questions:

- **Can I outsource this behavior?**

If the answer is "no," circle it. We will learn how to automate these behaviors in step four (testing your program).

If the answer is "yes," continue through the following questions:

- **Can I get someone to do this for me for free?**

Really brainstorm this. Is there someone that would be willing to help you out? Or someone that would be willing to swap services with you?

If the answer is "no," continue to the next question:

- **Can I get an app to do it for free, or for a small cost?**

If you can't get a person to do it for free, you may be able to get an app or another software program to do it for free. In fact, this is sometimes even better.

SOMETHING IS WRONG WITH OUR BRAINS.

The number of quality paid apps is insanely high. Sometimes, we have this weird psyche in our brains where we are fine to go out to lunch every day (often spending between $7-$15), but we can't bring ourselves to buy a $4.99 app.

For the love of everything, buy the $4.99 app! More often than not, it is a solid investment.

And, if you can buy an app to solve a legitimate problem or annoyance in your life, why would you not pay $4.99?!

If that's too expensive for you, then your "problem" isn't really that much of a problem.

Buying apps to help alleviate the more painful and difficult parts of my morning routine has been incredibly helpful for me.

But, if the answer to the above question is still "no," ask this final question:

- **Can I afford to hire someone to do it for me?**

There are certain things that we cannot get a person or an app to do for free (or even for a small price).

If that is the case, start considering the question, "Who can I hire?"

Whether you hire a virtual assistant, request a task on Fiverr, or outsource a project on Upwork, it is important to remember your motive.

Why are you choosing to automate your routines?

If your answer was anything other than "save money," then investing in any of these services will help you accomplish the outcome you desire.

I WANT A PERSONAL CHEF.

Here is a quick example of what this process might look like.

Let's say that in your ideal routine, you desire to have someone cook you a healthy breakfast that will be ready for you when you get home from a run.

Great.

Let's take that aspect of your ideal routine and filter it through the following questions.

- **Can I outsource this behavior?**

Yes, absolutely.

(If you're confused about what you cannot outsource, things like "go to the bathroom," "brush teeth," and "shower" would probably be included on the list.)

- **Can I get someone to do this for me for free?**

Maybe!

If you live with a spouse, you could ask them to help you.

If you live with roommates, you could ask them for help, too.

You might offer to help them with a service throughout the day, or tell them that you'll pay for the food if they make it (they would obviously make twice the amount and eat half).

You will be shocked at what happens when you ask kindly!

If you were asking your spouse, it might sound something like this:

"Hey honey, could I ask you a favor? I am really trying to eat better and I know that you are great at cooking healthily. When you make your breakfast, would you mind doubling it so that I can adopt your healthy eating habits?"

Hello, morning omelette.

- **Can I get an app to do it for free, or for a small cost?**

Let's say that you don't feel comfortable asking someone to help you (but, it is my opinion, it is always worth asking).

Or, maybe you don't have someone you could ask.

This means that we filter this element of our ideal routine through the next filter: "Can I get an app to do it for free, or for a small cost?"

The initial answer is "no." There is no app that can produce breakfast for you.

But, you may consider, "Is there an app that can help me know what healthy foods to eat for breakfast?"

Answer: yes!

(Check out the Forbes article, *"10 Top Apps For Eating Healthy."*)

You may feel satisfied making meals by yourself with guidance from an app, but you may still really want someone to make your meals for you.

This leads us to the final filter question.

- **Can I afford to hire someone to do it for me?**

You may do a search online for, "Personal chef in [city]."

You could also post a request on Craigslist: "In need of a chef to cook me breakfast every morning."

Also, make sure to post the request on your social media platforms as well, seeing who of your friends could accommodate your request.

If you're wondering how much to pay, simply do some research by asking, "How much should I pay my personal chef?"

You could even research, "How much should I charge? personal chef."

You'll come up with some good ideas of what to offer.

RINSE AND REPEAT.

When you begin to translate each item from your ideal routine to become an actual creation of your routine, you may not be required to go through all four filter questions.

You may find a perfect solution after the second question. Great! Move on!

But, let's say that you go through all of the filters, and none of them work.

That's alright.

Start by brainstorming, "What would be the next best thing?"

Remember, we're trying to create your most ideal routine.

You may not be able to create it 100% (to start), but the next best thing may only be a tier or two below what you originally wanted.

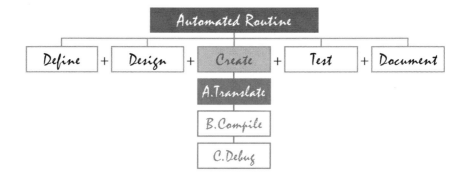

(COMPLETE ALL ACTION STEPS IN YOUR *Automate Your Routines, Guarantee Your Results WORKBOOK!*)

▌ ACTION STEPS

Suggested time to complete: 1.5 hours total

> *"It does not do well to dwell on dreams and forget to live, remember that."*
>
> *(J.K. Rowling, Harry Potter and the Sorcerer's Stone)*

Filter each item from your designed ideal routine through the following four questions:

- **Can I outsource this behavior?**

If "no," circle it. We will learn how to automate these in step four (testing your program).

If "yes," continue to filter it through the following questions:

- Can I get someone to do this for me for free?
- Can I get an app to do it for free, or for a small cost?
- Can I afford to hire someone to do it for me?

After you decide how to turn your ideal into a reality (or the next best thing), record it on a piece of paper or in a word processor.

TICK TOCK.

Next, add time parameters to each of these actions. How long will each step take? How do I need to readjust my morning to include each element of my ideal routine?

By the end of this step, you should have a nearly complete morning routine.

PITFALLS TO AVOID

- Don't be afraid to ask for things that you want!

Like I said earlier, you will be shocked to see how much you can get by simply asking.

If you don't believe me, **here is proof** (link in Workbook).

- If you're not sure what options are available, don't give up!

Research, research, research! Even two minutes of research will leave you infinitely more informed.

HELPFUL TOOLS:

- *Automate Your Routines, Guarantee Your Results Workbook*
- The internet (duh)

I've found that people have many similar needs when automating their morning routines, like waking up on time, actually waking up, and exercising. So here is a list of apps that I currently use to help automate my morning routine that might also help you:

- *Step Out Of Bed!*
  - Price: $1.99

As one who truly struggles waking up in the morning, this app has been a Godsend.

Here's how it works: the only way to turn off the alarm is to literally step out of bed!

Your phone knows this by tracking one of two things (whatever you decide when you set the alarm).

First, you can walk a certain number of steps. Only when you've walked that amount of steps will your alarm stop going off.

The second option (what I use), is that you have to take a picture that matches a picture you took when you set the alarm.

For example, when I first set my alarm, I took a picture of myself in my bathroom mirror.

Now, when my alarm rings in the morning, it will only turn off after I've taken a picture that looks similar to the one I took before.

This process of stepping out of bed and having to fulfill a task takes me out of the "oh, I don't need to be awake for three more hours" lie that I convince myself of every morning when I first wake up.

- *Headspace*
  - Price: Free, or $7.99/month for premium membership

To help even further with the truly concerning groggy state of mind I am in when I first wake up, I meditate.

It only takes ten minutes, but it forces me to focus, in a "your day is going to be great, you got this" kind of way.

- *Spotify*

- Free, or $9.99 for premium membership

I have a playlist that I use for my running route. I know how long each song is and where I need to be by the end of each song to be on track for my run time.

I also have a playlist that I use whenever I'm in the shower. I am a chronically long shower-er. I blame it on the two water heaters my family had growing up (first world problems, I know). But, when the playlist is over, my shower is over. It helps keep me on track.

- *Runkeeper*
  - Price: Free, or $39.99 for a premium membership

This is an app that tracks how far you've run, how fast you've run, and other helpful statistics.

Also, when you reach certain milestones, you get coupons for free and discounted stuff.

So, that's pretty neat.

- *Start Stretching*
  - Price: Free

A really simple stretching app that sends me reminders to, well, stretch! This is helpful, especially after my run, when sometimes, all I want to do is die because of that whole out-of-shape thing.

- *Sleep Cycle*
  - Price: Free, or $1.99 for premium membership

Instead of giving this app a specific time to wake you up, it will wake you up during a certain time interval when you are in your lightest sleep.

This will help you to be less groggy when you wake up.

It's amazing, it just didn't work for my particular routine.

Why did I stop using it? Because if my phone is by my bed, rather than on the other side of my room, I am absolutely doomed. There is no way I am waking up.

Some people are more disciplined than me, and thus, this may work for you.

B. COMPILE YOUR PROGRAM

Suggested time to complete: 30 minutes total

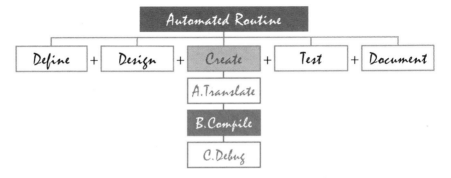

Compiling your program consists of going back through and finding any errors or holes in your routine.

With your routine in hand, go through each part of your routine, step by step.

Because you're creating your morning routine, you will start by lying in your bed.

Then, you'll walk through each part of your routine, as if it were the morning.

So, after lying in your bed, you will go and turn off your alarm.

Then, you will walk into the bathroom.

If the next step in your routine is to brush your teeth, you don't necessarily need to brush your teeth. Simply act as if you were.

As you do this, you will start to notice parts of your routine that you have to improvise because they haven't been defined.

If you are having to improvise, your routine is incomplete.

You need to make sure that you know each, exact step that you need to take to make your routine a success!

Here is an example of my routine. Notice how obnoxiously specific it is:

(For context, I've just returned from my run.)

- Go to bathroom
- Put headphones in bathroom drawer
- Push play on audiobook
- Fill mug by sink with cold water
- Drink the whole mug
- Wash face with face wash
- Remove remaining makeup with a makeup wipe
- Etc.

Are you starting to see how there are no gaps in my routine?

A poorly written schedule might be:

- Go to bathroom
- Get ready for the day

There is too much room for error or inconsistency!

We're trying to automate here, people!

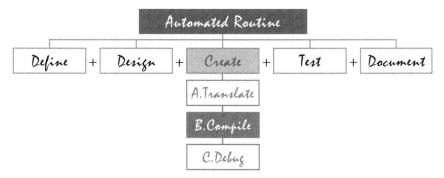

(COMPLETE ALL ACTION STEPS IN YOUR *Automate Your Routines, Guarantee Your Results WORKBOOK!*)

▓ ACTION STEPS

Suggested time to complete: 30 minutes total

"Originality depends on new and striking combinations of ideas."
(Rosamund Harding)

- Go through your entire routine. Pay attention to where you need to improvise, or where your routine is too ambiguous.

- Revise your routine to fill the holes.

▓ PITFALLS TO AVOID

- If some things simply will not work with your schedule, then create the next best solution.

You will have to modify. Remember, modifying doesn't necessarily mean downgrading. It can mean revising, or finding a way that is actually better for you!

ACCOMMODATE THE THUNDERS.

For example, after experiencing my routine a few times, I realized that I hated standing up while getting ready (I mentioned this earlier).

So, I modified my routine.

I added a "move chair from room to bathroom" step right after I got home from my run.

It was an extra step, but because I had a chair to sit on while I did my hair and makeup, my hair and makeup process went much faster.

If you need to modify, then modify!

HELPFUL TOOLS:

- *Automate Your Routines, Guarantee Your Results Workbook*
- *Timer+* (if you're needing to time out your routine, this is my favorite timer app)

C. DEBUG YOUR PROGRAM

Suggested time to complete: 2 hours total

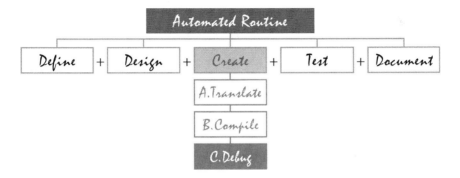

To debug means to declutter!

Now that you've gone through your routine, you've probably identified some areas of your life that are messy.

Your drawers may be out of control.

Your clean laundry may not have a designated place.

You may find that it's hard to locate your breakfast foods because your fridge is a hot mess.

What should you do?

Declutter!

Everything!

Anything that will not help you to implement your routines should be discarded.

Going through these questions as you declutter will help you determine what to do:

- Will this item help me fulfill my routine?

If "yes," ask:

- Is there anything I could do to make this item more easily accessible to make my routine run more smoothly?

If "no," ask:

- Can I eliminate this item/throw it away?

If "no," ask:

- Can I store this item?

If "no," ask:

- Can I arrange this item so that it doesn't interfere with my routine?

I guarantee that the answer to at least one of those questions will be "yes."

Don't allow your routine automation to be hindered because you were too lazy to discard things that weren't necessary.

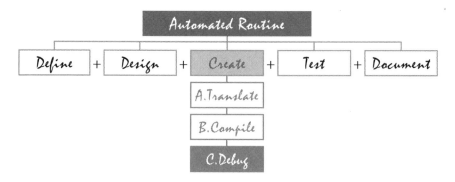

(COMPLETE ALL ACTION STEPS IN YOUR *Automate Your Routines, Guarantee Your Results WORKBOOK!*)

▊ ACTION STEPS

Suggested time to complete: 2 hours total

> *"Adapt what is useful, reject what is useless, and add what is specifically your own."*
> (Bruce Lee)

- Declutter every area that is accessed during your morning routine.

As you declutter, ask yourself the following questions about each item:

- Will this item help me fulfill my routine?

If "yes," ask:

- Is there anything I could do to make this item more easily accessible to make my routine run more smoothly?

If "no," ask:

- Can I eliminate this item/throw it away?

If "no," ask:

- Can I store this item?

If "no," ask:

- Can I arrange this item so it doesn't interfere with my routine?

▊ PITFALLS TO AVOID

- Make decisions quickly.

I recommend that you allow two hours for this task. But, you could honestly do it in about thirty minutes.

Do not get nostalgic. Do not get overwhelmed. Do not get all "I need to hold onto everything because my grandchildren will want to know what hairbrush I used in 2016"-esque on me.

▌ HELPFUL TOOLS:

- *Automate Your Routines, Guarantee Your Results Workbook*
- *This Spotify playlist* (link in Workbook)

Cleaning (debugging, decluttering, whatever you want to call it) is always easier when you've got some good jams.

Listen to my epic "Cleaning" playlist. Not to brag, but this is a great playlist (link in Workbook).

Disagree if you want, but don't tell me about it. Mmmkay?

▌ 4. TEST THE PROGRAM

Suggested time to complete: usually four to seven days to automate your routine

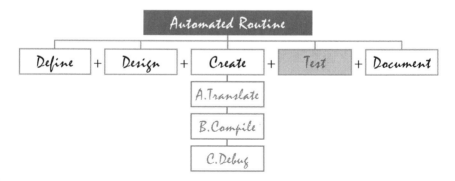

Now that the work is done, let's start to reap the results!

Give it a go!

Simply start running the program you've created.

Remember these guidelines when testing your solution:

- You must follow the routine in the same order. Do not skip over steps on purpose, and do not change the order of your routine.

- If you accidentally skip a step, stop yourself, and start the whole routine over. This will help your brain and body to truly automate the routines you're putting into place.

If you implement your program every day, it typically only takes about four to seven days for it to become second nature so the behaviors occur without conscious thought.

But, as you go through, know that you will likely find more holes in your routine.

Not a problem, simply fill the holes!

Add things that will help automate your routines, and eliminate those things that won't!

ELLEN IS MY WEAKNESS.

Let me give an example.

In the mornings, I found that right after I woke up, I was distracted by my phone. When I went into my bathroom to get ready for the day, I would sit in my chair, and, instead of washing my face to start my morning routine, I would whip out that lovely iPhone of mine.

I would immediately check my social media accounts and email. What resulted was a wasted twenty to twenty-five minutes every single morning.

Six Ellen Degeneres giveaway videos later (what, can you blame me?), I was starting my routine late. I had just woken up and my routine had already been derailed.

So, what did I do?

I bought a stress ball. You know, the kind that are filled with gel.

I then added two new steps into my morning routine after I turned off my alarm:

1. Put phone in bathroom drawer.
2. Pick up stress ball.

It's interesting. In most situations, you really only need one hand to get ready for the day.

By occupying my hand with something that didn't hold the distraction capabilities of a phone, I was able to eliminate that bad habit by simply writing it out of my routine!

Once that happened, the rest of my morning routine proceeded seamlessly.

It became automated.

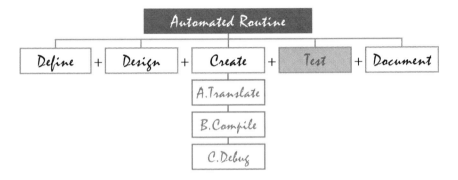

(COMPLETE ALL ACTION STEPS IN YOUR *Automate Your Routines, Guarantee Your Results WORKBOOK!*)

▌ ACTION STEPS

Suggested time to complete: however long your morning routine takes

> *"Good ideas are common, but those who are willing to take action and execute those ideas are far more rare."*
> (Pat Flynn, Will It Fly?)

- Run your program! Go through it in the exact order that you wrote it out. If you accidentally skip a step, start your routine over. Remember, we're trying to program your routine here.

- If you need to modify, then modify!

PITFALLS TO AVOID

- Giving up

The first few days are slightly tedious. You'll think, "Ugh, this takes forever." Or, "Why does it matter what order I do these things in if they all end up getting done?"

Remember, we are automating here! We are eliminating the need to use any extra brain power on these behaviors (allowing you to use that brain power for more worthwhile activities).

I must caution you: if you do not follow this automating system, you will fall back into your own habits.

Why?

Because you're relying on your willpower rather than an automated system.

And, willpower is just not reliable.

So, follow the system, won't you?

HELPFUL TOOLS:

- *Automate Your Routines, Guarantee Your Results Workbook*
- *Productive app*
  - Price: Free, or $3.99 for premium membership

There are a lot of apps out there that have varying versions of to-do lists, but for the purpose of routine automation, this one is my favorite.

You can insert as many tasks as you want, and then you can assign them to whatever time of the day you want.

You get reminders.

And, wow - isn't it just satisfying to check things off?

I knew that if I didn't have my list in front of me every morning, I wouldn't actually follow through with my plan.

This app has allowed me to see every step that I need to take.

115

5. DOCUMENT YOUR PROGRAM

Suggested time to complete: 5-15 minutes

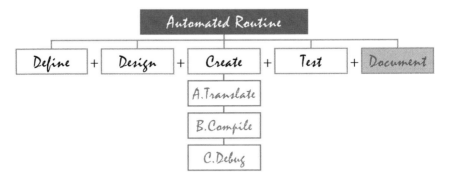

It is possible that you've already completed this step.

Throughout this whole process, you should have been writing down your routine.

Some of you will have every step written down nicely in a Word document.

Some of you may have printed it out, framed it, and hung it on your wall.

That's great.

This step isn't for you.

This step is for those people who wrote their routine out on a piece of paper, or a napkin, or in a random note in their phone.

This step is also for people who have everything written down and stored in a place where they will absolutely never see it again.

Your routine must be clearly documented and visible!

When your actions are clearly written down, they're solidified.

And, when they're visible (as in, you can actually see what you've written down), there is an added element of accountability.

When you make your routine visible, there are two things that you can display.

- You can either display your exact routine
- Or, you can display the "why" behind your routine (see Chapter 5).

WELCOME TO MY CRIB.

I've done a combination of both.

After writing out my morning routine, I printed it and then put it in a binder where I do my daily planning. That way, I can reference it when I need to, and am reminded of the morning routine I've automated.

I also have each step written out, and sent to me, via the Productivity app on my iPhone.

But, I also display the "why" behind my routine automation.

To quickly describe my "why" for automating my routines, I wanted to increase in both my diligence and virtue.

So, to display that, I had a quick logo drafted for me on Fiverr.

I said, "I want a logo, or image, that represents someone striving for diligence and virtue."

Here is what came back:

Since the development of my spirituality is a motivating factor in my desire to increase in diligence and virtue, I thought this was perfect.

I display the image on many different mediums to help me remember the "why" behind my routine automation.

For example, I have the image as the background on my phone.

I have it hanging as a keychain from my rearview mirror.

And, I have it printed on one of my credit cards.

These elements of documentation serve as a reminder for why I choose to automate certain routines in my life.

It also pushes me to focus more intently on things of greater importance.

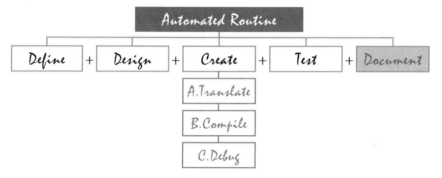

(COMPLETE ALL ACTION STEPS IN YOUR *Automate Your Routines, Guarantee Your Results WORKBOOK!*)

▌ACTION STEPS

Suggested time to complete: 5-15 minutes total

> *"If you're aware enough to give yourself a choice, you can choose to look differently. You get to decide what has meaning and what doesn't."*
> (David Foster Wallace)

118

- Clearly write out your morning routine in your *Automate Your Routines, Guarantee Your Results Workbook*, or any word processor.
- Choose to display one of the following in a location where you will regularly see it:
  - The actual list of your routine
  - An image or word that represents the "why" behind your routine

PITFALLS TO AVOID

Creating your routine automation program and then not displaying it is like creating a painting and hanging it up in the back of your closet.

Display your work! It will motivate you for the first few days of implementing your routine. Besides, who knows who else you will inspire through your efforts.

HELPFUL TOOLS:

- *Automate Your Routines, Guarantee Your Results Workbook*
- *Fiverr*
  - Get a logo or design made (to represent your "why") for only $5
- *Zazzle*
  - A website that allows you to print custom images on keychains, mugs, sweatshirts, etc.

SUGGESTED SCHEDULE

Here is how I recommend breaking up the five-step formula:

Day 1: Follow step one and two of the automation formula.

Define the problem
Design a solution

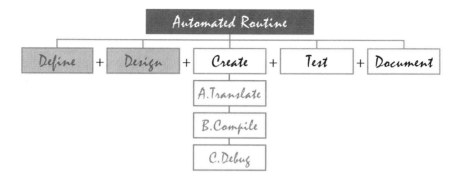

Day 2: Follow the first and second part of step three.

Create your program

- Part 1: Translate your solution
- Part 2: Compile your program

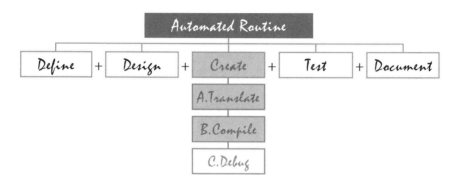

Day 3: Follow part three of step three of the formula.

Create your program

- Part 3: Debug your program

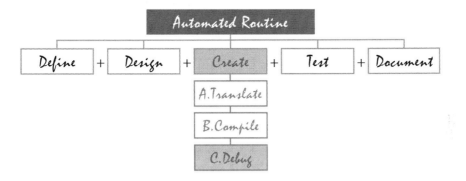

Day 4: Follow step four and five of the formula.

Test your program
Document your program

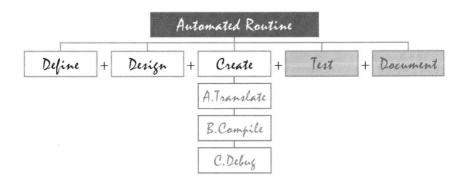

Day 5, 6, and 7: Repeat step four of the formula until it becomes automated.

Test your solution, test your solution, test your solution!

MORNING, EVENING, AND THEN EATING.

To the forward thinkers out there, I also suggest that you first automate your morning routine, then your evening routine, and then your eating routines.

This way, you won't overload your system by uploading too many programs too quickly.

Luckily, you will find that after you automate your morning routine, your brain's ability to automate your evening routine and your eating routine (or any other routine, for that matter) will increase significantly.

DREAMS COME TRUE.

Just think - within one week, you will have automated anywhere from 20 to 200 habits, depending on how elaborate your morning routine is.

One week!

The next week, as you implement your evening routine, you will have automated 20 to 200 more habits!

The week after, as you implement your eating routine, you will have automated 20 to 200 more habits!

For you former Mathletes (#anothershoutout), we're talking 2.8 to 28 new habits each day, all because you designed your program up front and then automated it.

HOW TO MOVE FORWARD.

If you'd rather implement your morning routine for the next week before reading on, do so.

Personally, I'm more of the, "let me read the whole book and then I'll do my thing" type of girl.

Whatever you choose to do is up to you.

NEXT STEP?

Evening routine! Flip the page and we'll tackle it together.

BUT WAIT!

Make sure to take advantage of all of the tools listed throughout the chapter. Before you move on, I want to make sure you have accessed everything available to you!

Automate Your Routines, Guarantee Your Results Workbook Resources and References

To download these tools, visit
http://www.booksbykathryn.com/ayrgyrresource.

CHAPTER 7:

AUTOMATE YOUR EVENING ROUTINE

*If you're wanting to get started right away (or you're revisiting this chapter), make sure to download the **Automate Your Routines, Guarantee Your Results Workbook.***

Morning routine automated? Check.

Now let's tackle your evening routine.

STOP KILLING YOURSELF.

If you're thinking, "Meh, it's okay. As long as my morning routine is set, I'll be fine," then you're doomed.

I'll also guess that you love watching Netflix and scrolling through Facebook before bed.

May I direct you to the Huffington Post article, *"Reading On A Screen Before Bed Might Be Killing You."*

Sorry, things got pretty heavy there.

But, hey, someone needed to tell you.

Evening routines serve as the final bookend to your day. It is the official retirement of the activities, stresses, successes, and downfalls that you experienced that day.

Here is a glimpse of the goodness awaiting you once you automate your evening routine:

● **Namaste**

Your mornings will be significantly more calm, productive, and welcomed.

If you haven't already guessed, the success of your morning routine is highly dependent upon the success of your evening routine.

You could have gone through the perfect five-step formula and crafted the most amazing morning routine.

You could plan to wake up at 6:30am and take on the world before you leave for work.

But if you continue to go to bed at 2:00am, your routine simply is not going to work.

(Or, you'll eventually start walking around like a zombie because four hours of sleep is simply ridiculous.)

A consistent evening routine will not only aid your morning routine, but it will also help you in other facets of your life.

● **Say goodbye to 5-Hour Energy**

Your body and mind will feel full and refreshed.

Unfortunately, there is not a switch that can turn your mind off. And, for people like me, who are thinking a million miles an hour and analyzing things all the time, this can be problematic.

Sometimes, I am afraid to go to sleep because I'm on the verge of figuring something out and don't want to miss it.

This results in me swirling thoughts around and battling the urge to get out of bed to write them down.

This battle continues until suddenly, three hours have passed.

Sure, I may have had a good idea.

But I am exhausted.

I get back into bed after writing the idea down, and still seem to struggle to fall asleep because this new business or book idea or blog article continues to occupy my mind.

This cycle will burn you out.

I know it did for me.

JUST KEEP SWIMMING, JUST KEEP SWIMMING.

Our bodies crave consistency.

By providing our bodies and minds with an automatic evening routine, it declares that the day is over.

And our bodies and minds react to that declaration. This means that you can actually fall asleep when you want to fall asleep.

The physical and mental benefits to automating your evening routine are immeasurable.

Now let's get to automating!

> **(Note:** This chapter and the next (Automate Your Eating Routines) will be less saturated with "how to" information since an in-depth overview of the five-step formula can be found in Chapter 4, and a very thorough example of automating your morning routine can be found in Chapter 6.
>
> Instead, this and the following chapter will include more examples of what particular evening and eating routines could look like. I'm simply trying to get out of your way so you can start creating and living your routines, rather than continue to read about them.)

1. DEFINE THE PROBLEM

Suggested time to complete: 10 minutes total

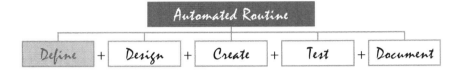

You know how this works.

As you focus on the current state of your evening routine, answer the following questions:

- **What is boring about your evening routine?**

Example: I believe that having to floss is not only the most boring thing ever, but also disgusting. I know it's my own saliva, but it's still gross. By the end of the experience, I've got slobber all over my face and hands.

- **What is stressful about your evening routine?**

Example: I always try to plan for the next day the night before, but doing so stresses me out. I just end up fussing over all of the things I need to accomplish the next day.

- **What is difficult about your evening routine?**

Example: Sometimes, the thought of getting ready for bed makes me feel exhausted. So, I do the only logical thing to do (#not), and stay up even later to avoid the routine entirely. It's an awful, stupid cycle.

Do not suppress any thoughts that come to your mind, regardless of how trivial or monumental the problems may seem. Write down everything you can think of!

Set a timer, and really force yourself to discover the annoyances and difficulties that you endure.

If you're stuck, here are some common complaints about evening routines:

- "I have a hard time falling asleep."

- "I'm embarrassed to say this, but brushing my teeth is the biggest struggle of my life."

- "Sometimes, I don't want to go to bed because I feel like nighttime is the only time I have to myself."

- "When I get ready for bed, I play music from my phone. Oftentimes, this results in me getting distracted by my phone, which means my evening routine turns into a forty-five minute ordeal. Ugh."

- "I become hungry whenever I think about going to bed. I hate it."

Remember, identifying these problems will help you to know how to design your ideal routine to eliminate these obstacles.

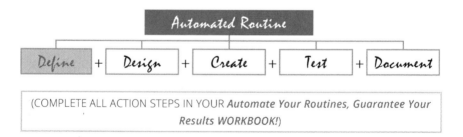

(COMPLETE ALL ACTION STEPS IN YOUR *Automate Your Routines, Guarantee Your Results* WORKBOOK!)

ACTION STEPS

Suggested time to complete: 10 minutes

> *"If I had an hour to solve a problem and my life depended on the solution, I would spend the first fifty-five minutes determining the proper question to ask, for once I know the proper question, I could solve the problem in less than five minutes."*
>
> *(Albert Einstein)*

Give at least three answers to the following questions:

1. What is boring about my evening routine?
2. What is stressful about my evening routine?
3. What is difficult about my evening routine?

PITFALLS TO AVOID

1. Remember, no problem is too small or too big.

Write it all down.

FOMO, AMIRITE?

Want to know one problem I identified within my evening routine?

"I suffer from FOMO."

For those of you unaware with the acronym FOMO, it stands for "fear of missing out."

I literally used to experience emotional angst because I felt like I was missing out on experiences by going to bed at a decent hour.

But, I wrote a routine that eliminated that fear. I still go to bed early. And, guess what I've missed out on so far? Nothing!

Because I haven't missed out on anything, it has led me to believe in one of two possible conclusions:

1. I don't need to be afraid of missing out.
2. Or, I have really boring friends.

HELPFUL TOOLS:

- *Automate Your Routines, Guarantee Your Results Workbook*

2. DESIGN A SOLUTION

Suggested time to complete: 45 minutes total

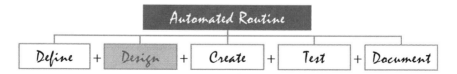

If you recall from the previous chapters, when you design your solution, you-

1. Brain dump all possible components to your perfect evening routine

2. Order your brain dump into a more routine-like format

READY OR NOT...

Here's another look into my brain. Remember, I am answering the question, "What would my ideal evening routine look like?"

- I want someone to read to me every night before I go to bed.

- I want someone to take away my computer from me so I am not distracted by the internet.

- I want someone to pick out my clothes for the next day.

- I want someone to lay out my workout clothes for the next morning.

- I want my room to be pitch black and silent when I go to sleep.

- I want three pillows instead of one.

- I want to go to bed feeling confident about what is going to happen the next day.

- I want to go to bed feeling confident that my most important relationships are stable.

You then take these ideas and organize them into a series of steps that comprise a routine.

For example:

1. Go to my bathroom.

2. Before doing anything to get ready for bed, have a personal assistant text/call back everyone that I hadn't responded to that day.

3. Confirm the outfit that someone has picked out for me for the next day.

4. Confirm the workout clothes that someone has picked out for me for the next day.

5. Etc.

Remember, you're creating your most ideal routine!

ARE YOUR FORGETTING SOMETHING?

So you don't forget anything, here are some typical elements that comprise evening routines:

- Changing clothes
- Washing face/teeth
- Connecting with a higher power
- Preparing for next day
- Connecting with loved ones
- Reading
- Sleeping

Automated Routine

| *Define* | + | *Design* | + | *Create* | + | *Test* | + | *Document* |

(COMPLETE ALL ACTION STEPS IN YOUR *Automate Your Routines, Guarantee Your Results WORKBOOK!*)

ACTION STEPS

Suggested time to complete: 45 minutes total

> *"She was becoming herself and daily casting aside that fictitious self which we assume like a garment with which to appear before the world."*
> *(Kate Chopin, The Awakening)*

Complete the following two tasks:

- Eliminate all distractions and do a twenty minute brain dump, answering the question, "What would my ideal evening routine look like?"

Remember, for this exercise, think as if you have all of the time, money, and resources in the world.

- With distractions still eliminated, take twenty-five minutes to revise your brain dump and organize your brainstormings into a chronological order.

Fill in any holes and flesh out any ideas. The goal is to have a complete, perfect routine by the end of the twenty-five minutes.

PITFALLS TO AVOID

- **Don't feel selfish or guilty about what you wish your ideal evening routine to be. Just write it down!**

I mean, I literally want someone (preferably Adele), to sing me to sleep. And, I'm not talking a recording. I'm saying that I wish that the British goddess herself would come sing me to sleep every night. That's a completely outrageous request. But, you better believe I wrote it down.

- **Don't justify ideas away.**

See the Adele answer above.

- **Don't feel discouraged.**

Once again, the current status of your evening routine is going to vary significantly from your ideal evening routine.

That is okay! We're designing what to work toward!

Brian Tracy, an expert in organizational and individual development said, "All successful people, men and women, are big dreamers. They imagine what their future could be, ideal in every respect, and then they work every day toward their distant vision, that goal or purpose."

That's what we're doing here.

HELPFUL TOOLS:

- *Automate Your Routines, Guarantee Your Results Workbook*
- *Pen and paper*
- *WriteRoom app* (blocks out the whole screen as you write)
- *Freedom app* (blocks out the internet for however long you'd like)
- *Timer+ app* (my favorite timer tool)

Optional tools

- If you're struggling (and I mean really struggling), check out these people's evening routines to spark some ideas.
  - *"The Evening Routines of the Most Successful People"* (link in Workbook)
  - *"5 Nighttime Routines of Successful Entrepreneurs"* (link in Workbook)

133

3. CREATE YOUR PROGRAM

Suggested time to complete: 4 hours total

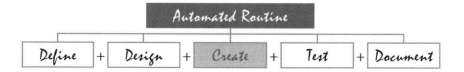

It is time to take your routine blueprints and transform them into your reality.

Creating your program consists of three parts.

PROUD OF YOU.

Because you've already done this once, and have already debugged (or decluttered) a lot of areas in your home already, this step will take significantly less time!

A. TRANSLATE YOUR PROGRAM

Suggested time to complete: 1.5 hours total

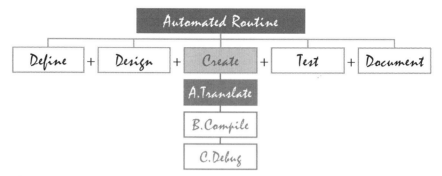

This is where you'll take your ideal routine, and, through a series of questions and research, create a program that is as close to your ideal as possible.

Here, you'll essentially create the rough draft of your ideal, perfect routine.

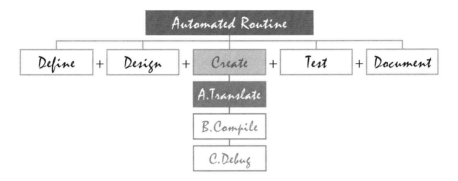

(COMPLETE ALL ACTION STEPS IN YOUR *Automate Your Routines, Guarantee Your Results WORKBOOK!*)

ACTION STEPS

Suggested time to complete: 1.5 hours total

> *"Creativity is just connecting things."*
> *(Steve Jobs)*

Filter each item from your designed ideal routine through the following four questions:

- Can I outsource this behavior?

If "no," circle it. We will learn how to automate these in step four (testing your program).

If "yes," continue to filter it through the following questions:

- Can I get someone to do this for me for free?
- Can I get an app to do it for free, or for a small cost?
- Can I afford to hire someone to do it for me?

After you decide how to turn your ideal into a reality (or the next best thing), record it on a piece of paper or in a word processor.

135

(If you'd like to see an example of how to go through this process, refer back to Chapter 4, where, I go through, in detail, how to filter each item of your routine through these questions.)

TIME AFTER TIME.

Next, add time parameters to each of these actions. How long will each step take? How do I need to readjust my evening to include each element of my ideal routine?

By the end of this step, you should have a nearly complete evening routine.

PITFALLS TO AVOID

- As stated previously, good things come to those that ask!

Ask for help! And, ask for free help! You'll be shocked to see what you'll receive.

- Research, research, research!

Not sure what apps are available? Search!

Struggling with getting your mind to turn off? Research what solutions have worked for other people!

Can't get your kids to go to bed when you want them to? Ask other parents what they've done!

HELPFUL TOOLS:

- *Automate Your Routines, Guarantee Your Results Workbook*
- The internet (duh)

So you know what works for me, here is a list of apps that I currently use to help automate my evening routine:

- *Relax Melodies*
  - Price: Free, or $9.99 for premium membership

This is an app that plays soothing sounds to help you fall asleep.

You can also access a series of meditations that are geared towards luring you into sleep.

Among my favorite meditations are "Sleep into Well-Being," "Sleep Therapy for Deep Calm," "Reclaim Peaceful Sleep," and "Positive Dreaming."

If you're someone who struggles to turn your mind off, even after going through your consistent evening routine, this application is for you!

- *Freedom*
  - Price: $24.00 per year

This app shuts off the internet on your computer and phone. You can set up one-time sessions, or, like I do, you can program recurring sessions.

In my personal routine, I make sure that my internet shuts off at 10:00pm every night.

Removing the internet strips away 90% of the distraction that I would typically face to prevent me from not initiating my evening routine.

This app has completely changed the way I live.

I am so grateful for it, and I recommend it to everyone I meet.

EVERYONE.

B. COMPILE YOUR PROGRAM

Suggested time to complete: 30 minutes total

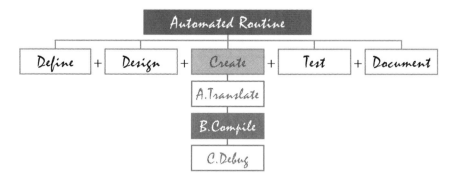

Compiling your program is like going through your routine the way a control-freak landlord goes through a cleaning check.

Don't allow any holes or ambiguity to infiltrate your routine!

Remember, to do this, you're actually going to go through your whole routine. Walk through it step by step.

And, anytime you are unsure of what to do, or have to improvise, you know that you've found a hole in your routine.

So, what should you do? Flesh it out.

Here is an example of part of my evening routine.

(For context, I've just finished washing my face.)

- 45 seconds of mouthwash
- Floss bottom teeth
- Floss top teeth
- Brush teeth
- Blistex on lips
- Lotion on left arm
- Lotion on right arm
- Etc.

There are no gaps!

"Get ready for bed" is not an acceptable evening routine.

Seriously, gag me.

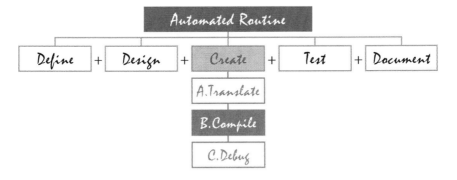

(COMPLETE ALL ACTION STEPS IN YOUR *Automate Your Routines, Guarantee Your Results WORKBOOK!*)

ACTION STEPS

Suggested time to complete: 30 minutes total

> *"I do not think there is any thrill that can go through the human heart like that felt by the inventor as he sees some creation of the brain unfolding to success...Such emotions make a man forget food, sleep, friends, love, everything."*
> (Nikola Tesla)

- Go through your entire routine. Pay attention to where you need to improvise, or where your routine is too ambiguous.

- Revise your routine to fill the holes.

PITFALLS TO AVOID

- If there are some things that just won't work with your schedule, then create the next best solution. You will have to modify. Such is life.

139

HELPFUL TOOLS

- *Automate Your Routines, Guarantee Your Results Workbook*
- *Timer+* (if you're needing to time out your routine, this is my favorite timer app)

C. DEBUG YOUR PROGRAM

Suggested time to complete: 2 hours total

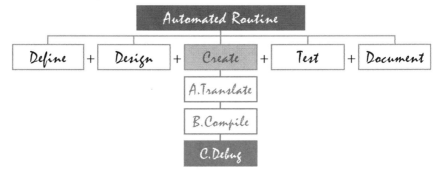

Don't sabotage your routine before you even start it.

Get everything out of the way that won't contribute to the success of your evening routine automation.

I'm serious. Everything!

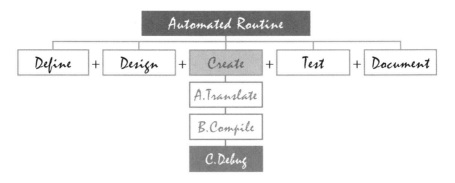

(COMPLETE ALL ACTION STEPS IN YOUR *Automate Your Routines, Guarantee Your Results WORKBOOK!*)

▌ACTION STEPS

Suggested time to complete: 2 hours total

> *"True happiness comes from the joy of deeds well done,*
> *the zest of creating things new."*
> *(Antoine de Saint-Exupery)*

- Declutter every area that is used during your evening routine.

As you declutter, ask yourself the following questions about each item:

- Will this item help me fulfill my routine?

If "yes," ask:

- Is there anything I could do to make this item more easily accessible to make my routine run more smoothly?

If "no," ask:

- Can I eliminate this item/throw it away?

If "no," ask:

- Can I store this item?

If "no," ask:

- Can I arrange this item so it doesn't interfere with my routine?

▌PITFALLS TO AVOID

- *Nostalgia is the enemy* (link in Workbook).

▌HELPFUL TOOLS:

- *Automate Your Routines, Guarantee Your Results Workbook*
- *This Spotify playlist* (link in Workbook)

Once again, for your listening pleasure, download the *Automate Your Routines, Guarantee Your Results Workbook* to get access to my "Cleaning" playlist on Spotify.

4. TEST THE PROGRAM

Suggested time to complete: usually four to seven days to automate your routine

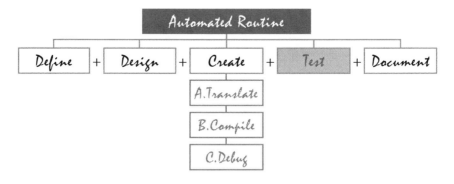

(COMPLETE ALL ACTION STEPS IN YOUR *Automate Your Routines, Guarantee Your Results WORKBOOK!*)

ACTION STEPS

Suggested time to complete: however long your evening routine takes

> *"So we beat on, boats against the current, borne back ceaselessly into the past."*
>
> *(F. Scott Fitzgerald, The Great Gatsby)*

- Run your program! Go through it in the exact order that you wrote it out. If you accidentally skip a step, start your routine over. Remember, we're trying to program our routines here.

- If you need to modify, then modify!

PITFALLS TO AVOID

- In the beginning, tedious isn't bad.

Here is some great news: if you've already worked to automate your morning routine, you won't struggle with this at all!

It is essential that you go through each step, in the correct order, every night. We're trying to get your brain to use as little conscious thought as possible, so, doing things in an identical order each night will help your mind and body to truly automate your evening routine.

HELPFUL TOOLS:

- *Automate Your Routines, Guarantee Your Results Workbook*
- *Productive app*
    - Price: Free, or $3.99 for premium membership

You've heard it all before, in fact, a chapter ago. I'm obsessed with this app.

5. DOCUMENT YOUR PROGRAM

Suggested time to complete: 5-15 minutes

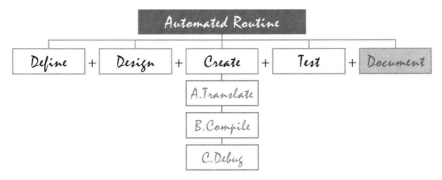

If you already completed this step when creating your morning routine, *watch this five second video* to celebrate (link in Workbook).

If you have not yet completed this portion of the formula, you know the drill!

(COMPLETE ALL ACTION STEPS IN YOUR *Automate Your Routines, Guarantee Your Results WORKBOOK!*)

ACTION STEPS

Suggested time to complete: 5-15 minutes total

> *"Paper is to write things down that we need to remember. Our brains are used to think."*
> *(Albert Einstein)*

- Clearly write out your evening routine in your **Automate Your Routines, Guarantee Your Results Workbook,** or any word processor.

- Choose to display one of the following in a location where you will regularly see it:

  - The actual list of your routine

  - An image or word that represents the "why" behind your routine

PITFALLS TO AVOID

- Not doing this step. Don't be that person.

HELPFUL TOOLS:

- *Automate Your Routines, Guarantee Your Results Workbook*
- *Fiverr*
  - Get a logo or design made (to represent your "why") for only $5
- *Zazzle*
  - A website that allows you to print custom images on keychains, mugs, sweatshirts, etc.

SUGGESTED SCHEDULE

For my suggestion on when to tackle each part of the five-step formula, see the schedule outlined at the end of the "Automate Your Morning Routine" chapter.

ALL ABOARD.

Next stop? Automating your eating routines!

THESE ARE BASICALLY PARTY FAVORS.

Make sure to take advantage of all of the tools listed throughout the chapter. Before you move on, I want to make sure you have accessed everything available to you!

Automate Your Routines, Guarantee Your Results Workbook
Resources and References

To download these tools, visit
http://www.booksbykathryn.com/ayrgyrresource.

CHAPTER 8:

AUTOMATE YOUR EATING ROUTINES

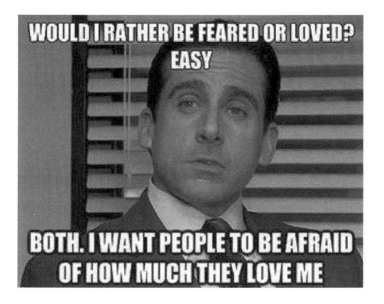

YO QUIERO TACO BELL.

This is how I feel about Crunchwrap Supremes from Taco Bell.

I am truly afraid of how much I love them.

If you've never tried one, I suggest you put down this book and go get one.

Then, obviously, come back to reading this book.

Now, do I know that Crunchwrap Supremes are extremely bad for me?

Yes.

But, somehow, before this whole "eating routine automation" thing, I kept getting lured in.

Was it because, for a long time, Taco Bell was the only restaurant anywhere remotely close to where I worked?

Was it because I had developed extremely bad taste and actually believed Taco Bell to be delicious? (This is a definite yes. Because I still think Taco Bell is delicious.)

Or, was it the irresistibly entertaining sayings printed on the outside of the Taco Bell hot sauce packets that always brought me back?

Whatever it was, it was taking over my life one processed-meat packed tortilla at a time.

WHEN REALITY SETS IN.

I was getting older, and was sadly becoming more aware that my high metabolism (a blessing from heaven) was going to slow down one day.

Also, I was tired of feeling awful.

And slow.

Generally sloth-like.

And my immune system is already unimpressive, so feeding it Taco Bell on the regular was definitely not contributing to improved health.

In addition to my Taco Bell obsession, I also ate out all the time.

The reason is probably because I am not a great cook.

I also don't enjoy cooking.

And I think it takes too long.

And the grocery store is one of the biggest annoyances of my life.

As you can see, things needed to change.

147

So, as I'm sure you can guess, I decided to automate my eating habits.

Cue the applause.

DISCLAIMER.

In case you haven't yet gathered this, let me preface this chapter by saying I am not a certified nutritionist.

With that said, I have done extensive research on how to automate eating behaviors.

Before I go into the nitty gritty of automating my eating routines (and help you to do the same), here are some more specific "why's" behind my desire to automate my eating routines.

- I did not want to be on a diet. I just wanted to be more consistent with my food choices.

- I never wanted to feel hungry.

- I never wanted to have to scramble to get food ready.

- I never wanted to feel guilty about what I was eating.

- I never wanted to waste time cooking, or be standing at my fridge thinking, "What am I going to eat today?"

If you have different dietary needs, you'll have to adjust your objectives. But for me, this was what I desired from my eating routines.

TONY HORTON, ANYONE?

I had previously completed the P90X program and had followed their food program pretty religiously.

And, I felt great!

But meals became the focus of my days. I had to cook and prepare and spend time learning how to make dishes I wasn't familiar with.

I hated it.

It consumed too much of my time.

And, even though I got better at cooking each of the meals, it was still too much time.

Thus, to automate my eating routines, I decided to really factor in the elimination of decision fatigue.

I decided that I would eat the same breakfast every day.

I decided that I would eat the same lunch every day.

And, I decided that I would eat the same dinner every day.

SOCIAL PROOF.

Before you think I'm crazy, please be aware that a lot of people do this.

Remember Jennifer Aniston and Courtney Cox who ate the same salad for lunch every day?

Tim Ferriss, the automation expert who we spoke about earlier, reports that he has eaten the same breakfast and lunch for over two years.

Why?

Because the automation benefits are huge (reduce decision fatigue, preserve willpower), and the health benefits are also profitable.

Reports show that people who eat the same meals every day consume fewer calories and more easily lose weight.

Also, their bodies learn to crave the few meals they actually eat.

For me, the primary benefit was the increase of time that I enjoyed.

But, that doesn't mean that I haven't lost weight (which I have), felt healthier (which I have), started having clearer and brighter skin (which I have), started craving only healthy foods - really just the three meals that I eat each day (which I have), and have saved hundreds and hundreds of dollars on food each month (which I have).

Let's get you automating your own eating routine.

Here we go!

1. DEFINE THE PROBLEM

Suggested time to complete: 10 minutes total

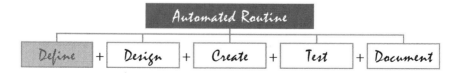

To start, brainstorm answers to these three questions (are these questions looking familiar, yet?)

- **What is boring about my eating routines?**

Example: I absolutely hate doing dishes. Because of this, I don't cook as often as I probably should.

- **What is stressful about my eating routines?**

Example: I never seem to have enough food, or food that I want, in my pantry. Because of that, I don't eat before I leave for the day, which means I starve until lunch.

- **What is difficult about my eating routine?**

Example: I never feel like I have enough time to make meals that are healthy.

Once again, set a timer and let all of your inner angst regarding your eating habits surface. Write it all down!

Here are some typical complaints about eating routines:

- "I don't have enough money to buy healthy food."

- "I hate how much money I spend eating out."

- "I am so bad at cooking that I have no other choice but to eat out."

- "I am so bad at planning meals and cooking that I never seem to have food in my house. Or, I have too much food and it all ends up going to waste."

- "I cannot control myself when it comes to food. I crave things that are unhealthy for me all the time."

Identify the components of your eating routine that are boring, stressful, or difficult, and then we'll work to automate an eating routine that will eliminate them from your life!

(COMPLETE ALL ACTION STEPS IN YOUR *Automate Your Routines, Guarantee Your Results WORKBOOK!*)

ACTION STEPS

Suggested time to complete: 10 minutes

"Whenever you find yourself on the side of the majority, it's time to pause and reflect."
(Mark Twain)

Give at least three answers to the following questions:

1. What is boring about my eating routine (consider breakfast, lunch, dinner, and snacking)?

2. What is stressful about my eating routine (consider breakfast, lunch, dinner, and snacking)?

3. What is difficult about my eating routine (consider breakfast, lunch, dinner, and snacking)?

PITFALLS TO AVOID

- Food seems to be a more sensitive subject than most. I believe the reason is because the results of our eating habits are manifested on our bodies. Even so, don't be shy about what you write down.

151

THE STRUGGLE IS REAL.

I used to buy a huge soda every single day.

Every single day.

It was insanely delicious.

It was also probably killing me, one cup of concentrated chemicals at a time.

I was embarrassed that a 24 oz. drink had such control over my behavior.

But, to be truthful, it did.

So, I wrote it down.

Write down everything!

HELPFUL TOOLS:

- *Automate Your Routines, Guarantee Your Results Workbook*

2. DESIGN A SOLUTION

Suggested time to complete: 45 minutes total

To automate your eating routines, we will follow the same pattern that we did to automate our morning and evening routines.

Thus, in designing a "perfect" eating routine solution, make sure to:

1. Brain dump all possible components of your perfect eating routine.

2. Order your brain dump into a routine-like format.

To give some examples of what this might look like, here is a brain dump from my experience of answering the question, "What would my ideal eating routine look like?"

- Always have my cupboards filled with healthy foods
- Never have to cook my own meals
- Waste no time preparing meals
- Truly enjoy what I eat every day
- Not feel guilt about what I eat every day
- Not feel restricted like I would on a diet

Now, taking these aspects and crafting them into a routine might look something like this:

1. After completing my morning routine, have a breakfast, that I have already approved, ready for me to eat
2. Say a prayer, thanking God for the food and the new day
3. Eat breakfast at kitchen table
4. While eating breakfast, use that time to connect with a family member via telephone
5. Spend only ten minutes eating breakfast
6. Have someone do the dishes for me

GOT EVERYTHING?

As you create your ideal eating routine, keep in mind some common elements that typically dictate eating routines:

- Planning what to eat
- Preparing your food
- Eating your food
- Addressing a higher power
- Completing an activity while eating (talking to a loved one, watching a video, reading, etc.)
- Cleaning up food

153

(COMPLETE ALL ACTION STEPS IN YOUR *Automate Your Routines, Guarantee Your Results WORKBOOK!*)

ACTION STEPS

Suggested time to complete: 45 minutes total

> *"Exceptions are not born. They are created."*
> (James Altucher)

Complete the following two tasks:

- Eliminate all distractions and do a twenty minute brain dump, answering the question, "What would my ideal eating routine look like (consider breakfast, lunch, dinner, and snacks)?"

Remember, for this exercise, think as if you have all of the time, money, and resources in the world!

- With distractions still eliminated, take twenty-five minutes to revise your brain dump and organize your brainstormings into a chronological order.

Fill in any holes and flesh out any ideas. The goal is to have a perfect routine by the end of the twenty-five minutes.

PITFALLS TO AVOID

- Don't feel selfish or guilty for what you write down! As Selena Gomez said, "The heart wants what it wants."
- Don't justify away ideas.
- Don't feel discouraged.

I DARE YOU TO TRY THIS.

I served a mission for my church in Los Angeles. We were paired up in companionships as we went about our work. At one point, I was paired with an exceptional girl. She was hilarious.

One morning, I got out of the shower and went to the kitchen to make breakfast.

When I entered the kitchen, I startled my companion. She tried to hide what she was making for breakfast.

"What are you eating?" I asked.

"Nothing!"

"Oh my gosh," I responded as I got a glimpse of what she was creating. "What are you making?!"

Turns out, my companion had a fancy for Wonder Bread sandwiches with mayonnaise and Oreo cookies.

I am not kidding.

Hilarious.

I guess she ate one almost every morning while I was in the shower.

Maybe you're at a point where you're eating Wonder Bread sandwiches with mayonnaise and Oreo cookies every morning.

You may have a steep road ahead of you, but there is still hope.

And, in case you were wondering, I never did try one of those sandwiches.

▌ HELPFUL TOOLS:

- *Automate Your Routines, Guarantee Your Results Workbook*
- *Pen and paper*
- *WriteRoom app* (blocks out the whole screen as you write)

- *Freedom app* (blocks out the internet for however long you'd like)
- *Timer+ app* (my favorite timer tool)

Optional tools

- If you're struggling (and I mean really struggling), check out these people's eating routines to spark some ideas.
  - *"Healthy Eating Habits"* (link in Workbook)
  - *"How to lose 100 pounds"* (link in Workbook)

3. CREATE YOUR PROGRAM

Suggested time to complete: 4 hours total

Now that we have your ideal eating routine set, let's transform it into a reality!

Remember, this step of the formula consists of three different parts: translating your solution, compiling your program, and debugging your program.

A. TRANSLATE YOUR SOLUTION

Suggested time to complete: 1.5 hours total

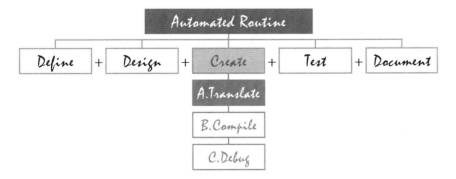

Here, you take your ideal routine and, through a series of questions, craft a program that is as close to your ideal as possible.

As an example, during this portion of the formula, I realized that I couldn't currently afford to get a chef to cook meals for me every day.

I was also pretty limited in my cooking skills and in the time I had to devote to learning cooking skills.

So, I thought to myself, "If I had to eat the same, simple meal every single day, could I do it?"

When I started with this extreme version of eating routine automation, I was a little skeptical. I had seen the success that had come from my morning and evening routines, but I was still unsure if it could work in this particular area of my life.

So, I made myself the promise, "If I absolutely start hating this food after two weeks, then I will switch up my eating routine."

Well, it has been nearly four months of me eating the same meals every day and I am happy to report that I am not sick of any of the meals I'm eating.

Nearly four months!

I know, I agree. It's awesome.

157

(COMPLETE ALL ACTION STEPS IN YOUR *Automate Your Routines, Guarantee Your Results WORKBOOK!*)

▍ACTION STEPS

Suggested time to complete: 1.5 hours total

> *"The best way to predict the future is to create it."*
> *(Peter Drucker)*

Filter each item from your designed ideal routine through the following four questions:

- Can I outsource this behavior?

If "no," circle it. We will learn how to automate these in step four (testing your program).

If "yes," continue to filter it through the following questions:

- Can I get someone to do this for me for free?
- Can I get an app to do it for free, or for a small cost?
- Can I afford to hire someone to do it for me?

After you decide how to turn your ideal routine into a reality (or the next best thing), record it on a piece of paper or in a word processor.

(If you'd like to see an example of how to go through this process, refer back to Chapter 4, where I go through, in detail, how to filter each item of your routine through these questions.)

WHAT TIME IS IT?

Next, add time parameters to each of these actions. How long will each step take? How do I need to readjust my morning and evening routines to include each element of my ideal eating routine?

By the end of this step, you should have a nearly complete eating routine.

PITFALLS TO AVOID

- Not asking because you're afraid of asking.
- Not researching 'cause lazy.

Unsure of what is a healthy balance of proteins, carbs, and fats for your age and gender? Research it!

Not sure what healthy foods you can take on the go? Research it!

Unsure of how to reduce your eating expenses by 50%? Research it!

HELPFUL TOOLS:

- *Automate Your Routines, Guarantee Your Results Workbook*
- The internet (duh)
- A people calendar
  - May I recommend you take Keith Ferazzi's advice to *never eat alone?*
  - Even though I live away from my family, I make sure to contact a specific member of my family during my lunch hour.
  - Figure out how to never eat alone in a way that best contributes to your goals and desired outcomes (refer to the "why" you determined earlier).
- If you're needing to unwind during a meal, and going outside or participating in a proactive activity just isn't an option, the *Evan Carmichael YouTube Channel* is gold.
  - It consists of videos that dissect influential people's top ten rules for success, along with other motivational videos. I'm obsessed.

As a side note, here is a current list of apps that I currently use to help automate my eating routine:

- *Productive*
  - Price: $3.99

Yes, I even enter my eating routines into this app. I seriously love it.

- *List Ease*
  - Price: Free

This is a handy little shopping list app. It allows you to scan the barcode of an item to automatically add it to your list.

It allows you to keep a list of foods that are in your pantry. When foods run out, you simply move them from your pantry list to your shopping list.

Finally, it also has a cute, animated logo that checks items off your list - which is always a bonus.

- *Eat This Much*
  - Price: $7/month

This website (not an app) provides a service that creates meal plans based on your diet goals. It can be customized according to your food preferences, budget, and schedule.

This was a great tool for me as I was researching what foods to actually eat.

B. COMPILE YOUR PROGRAM

Suggested time to complete: 30 minutes total

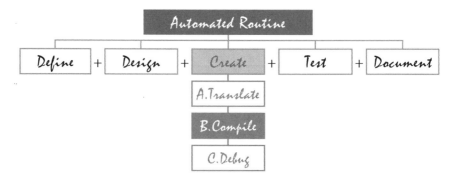

There cannot be any hiccups in your eating routine.

Here's an example of how specific your eating routine should be:

(This is after I've decided that I will eat egg whites with spinach and black beans for lunch every day.)

1. Put frying pan on front left burner

2. Turn burner on to 70% heat

3. Put a small pad of butter in the pan

4. Take spinach out of the fridge

5. Wash a small handful of spinach

6. Rip up the handful of spinach and put in the pan

7. Etc.

A vague plan of "make egg whites with spinach and black beans for lunch" simply won't cut it.

There is just too much ambiguity. What will happen when? What will you do to ensure that your frying pan is always clean? Will you use paper products or not?

Be specific!

GOING ON A TRIP, IN MY FAVORITE ROCKETSHIP.

As part of my eating routine, I schedule time every Saturday to go grocery shopping. By grouping my errands and completing them on the weekend, I am able to increase my productivity throughout the week.

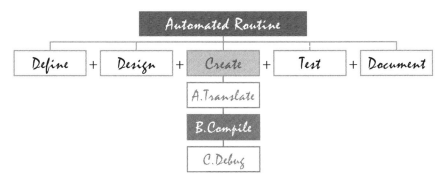

(COMPLETE ALL ACTION STEPS IN YOUR *Automate Your Routines, Guarantee Your Results WORKBOOK!*)

▌ACTION STEPS

Suggested time to complete: 30 minutes total

> *"There is no short cut to achievement. Life requires thorough preparation."*
> *(George Washington Carver)*

- Go through your entire routine. Pay attention to where you need to improvise, or where your routine is too ambiguous.

- Revise your routine to fill the holes.

▌PITFALLS TO AVOID

- If your ideal isn't possible, create the next best thing!

▌HELPFUL TOOLS

- *Automate Your Routines, Guarantee Your Results Workbook*

- *Timer+* (if you're needing to time out your routine, this is my favorite timer app)

▌ C. DEBUG YOUR PROGRAM

Suggested time to complete: 2 hours total

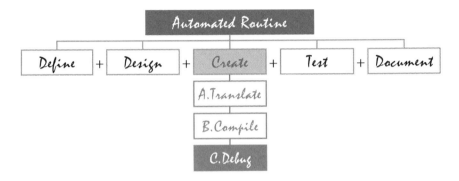

Get rid of anything that won't contribute to your eating routine automation.

And by "anything," I mean literally every food that isn't a part of your eating routine.

"Well, what if I just went to the grocery store?"

Give the food away.

"What if I live with other people?"

Then move all of their food to a completely different cabinet or pantry. Clear a space that is entirely your own. Do not let anyone (or any of their non-routine automated food) get near it.

You'll thank me later.

I'M SORRY (NOT REALLY) TO REPEAT MYSELF, BUT...

I know we used a similar example before, but it's important to bring it up again.

Let's say that you, in your routine automation, decide that you would like to eat a protein shake every morning for breakfast.

If you only have ingredients available to make a protein shake, what are you going to eat for breakfast every day?

You nailed it - a protein shake.

If you, along with your protein shake ingredients, also have Trix, bagels and cream cheese, and yogurt, your chances of eating a protein shake every morning for breakfast go down significantly.

Discard anything that will serve as a distraction to your eating routines.

Do not waste willpower on deciding what to eat. Decide once, and then automate it! The only way to truly automate your eating routine is if all other choices are eliminated.

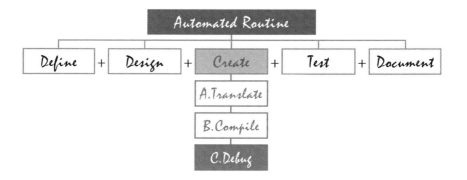

(COMPLETE ALL ACTION STEPS IN YOUR *Automate Your Routines, Guarantee Your Results WORKBOOK!*)

▌ ACTION STEPS

Suggested time to complete: 2 hours total

> *"The principle goal of education in the schools should be creating men and women who are capable of doing new things, not simply repeating what other generations have done."*
>
> (Jean Piaget)

- Declutter every area that is used during your eating routine.

As you declutter, ask yourself the following questions about each item:

- Will this item help me fulfill my routine?

If "yes," ask:

- Is there anything I could do to make this item more easily accessible to make my routine run more smoothly?

If "no," ask:

- Can I eliminate this item/throw it away?

If "no," ask:

- Can I store this item?

If "no," ask:

- Can I arrange this item so it doesn't interfere with my routine?

PITFALLS TO AVOID

- Don't get sidetracked.
- Don't be bothered by food you're giving away. Just rip off the Band-Aid.

Remember, we're looking for long-term, automated results. Decluttering is requisite.

HELPFUL TOOLS:

- *Automate Your Routines, Guarantee Your Results Workbook*
- *This Spotify playlist* (link in Workbook)

4. TEST THE PROGRAM

Suggested time to complete: usually four to seven days to automate your routine

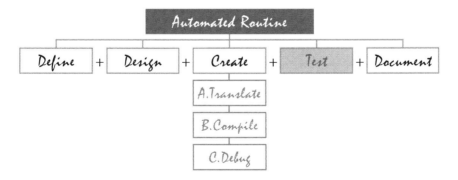

(COMPLETE ALL ACTION STEPS IN YOUR *Automate Your Routines, Guarantee Your Results WORKBOOK!*)

ACTION STEPS

Suggested time to complete: however long your eating routine takes

> *"At any rate, that is happiness; to be dissolved into something complete and great."*
> *(Willa Cather, My Antonia)*

- Run your program! Go through it in the exact order that you wrote it out. If you accidentally skip a step, start your routine over.

- If you need to modify, then modify!

PITFALLS TO AVOID

- In the beginning, the fact that going through each step in its exact order feels tedious isn't actually bad. It helps to program both your body and your brain, a little like muscle memory!

HELPFUL TOOLS:

- *Automate Your Routines, Guarantee Your Results Workbook*
- *Productive app*
  - Price: $3.99

Yep. The best task/to-do app ever!

5. DOCUMENT YOUR PROGRAM

Suggested time to complete: 5-15 minutes

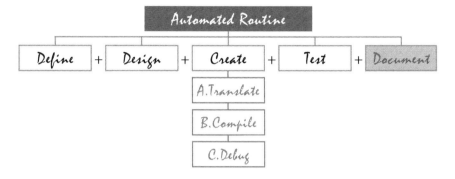

If you've already finished this step, I'm so proud of you.

tear

Y'all are growing up so fast.

(COMPLETE ALL ACTION STEPS IN YOUR *Automate Your Routines, Guarantee Your Results WORKBOOK!*)

ACTION STEPS

Suggested time to complete: 5-15 minutes total

"One must be careful of books, and what is inside them, for words have the power to change us."

(Cassandra Clare, The Infernal Devices)

- Clearly write out your eating routine in your ***Automate Your Routines, Guarantee Your Results*** Workbook, or any word processor.

- Choose to display one of the following in a location where you will regularly see it:

  - The actual list of your routine

  - An image or word that represents the "why" behind your routine

▊ PITFALLS TO AVOID

- Not making your visual reminder visual. C'mon guys. Don't be like that.

▊ HELPFUL TOOLS:

- *Automate Your Routines, Guarantee Your Results Workbook*
- *Fiverr*
    - Get a logo or design made (to represent your "why") for only $5
- *Zazzle*
    - A website that allows you to print custom images on keychains, mugs, sweatshirts, etc.

▌ SUGGESTED SCHEDULE

For my suggestion on when to tackle each part of the five-step formula, see the schedule outlined at the end of the "Automate Your Morning Routine" chapter.

I'M GOING TO DISNEYLAND!

We've worked through automating your morning, evening, and eating routines. How are you going to celebrate?

Before you go to Disneyland, read the last chapter for some final tactics to achieve flawless routine automation!

BECAUSE I LIKE YOU.

From one routine automationist to another, once again, here are some tools you'll find useful.

Automate Your Routines, Guarantee Your Results Workbook Resources and References

To download these tools, visit ***http://www.booksbykathryn.com/ayrgyrresource.***

CHAPTER 9:

THE FINAL COUNTDOWN

We've come a long way.

But we've still got some ground to cover in this last chapter.

Namely, we'll address what's possible for you now that you've learned how to automate your routines, and what your next steps should be.

WHAT ARE YOU DOING HERE?

The fact that you've read this book indicates a few things:

1. You are hungry to change and improve.
2. You now have the tools to automate your morning, evening, and eating routines.
3. You might be my mom (Hi, Mom).

Honestly, you're miles ahead of everyone else who talks about getting their life in order.

Follow the five-step formula outlined in this book and you will never, ever, be the person who can only talk the talk.

In fact, you'll start to cringe when you hear people say things like, "Yeah, I really need to wake up early so I can work on writing that book I've always wanted to write."

Or, "I keep making the goal to go to bed on time, but it never works."

Or finally, "I just wish I had a personal chef to come cook for me all the time. Then I would eat healthily!"

After hearing those comments, you'll want to take these poor people by the shoulders to try and shake them out of their delusional state!

(Just remember to be gentle.)

If only they realized how easily their dreams could become a reality!

But we were once routine automation ignorant fools ourselves.

In fact, when you started reading this book, it's probable that you came in with inconsistent, sub-par, or non-existent morning, evening, and eating routines.

But by combining the principles of computer programming, along with the science of decision fatigue, you've taken the elements of those routines that you hate the most, and have automated them.

TELL ME HOW GREAT I AM.

Because it's nice to admire the work you've done (or are about to do), let's recap what you've experienced so far, shall we?

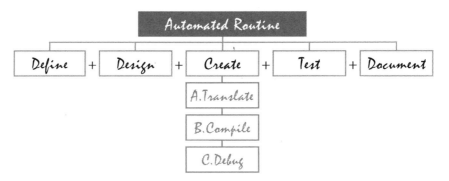

By following the five-step formula, you've first identified the problems that have infiltrated your routines. And, by fleshing out the boring, stressful, and difficult parts of your routines, you took the first step in eliminating them.

Then, imagining you had all of the resources, time, and money in the world, you crafted your ideal routine in the second step of the formula.

As you know, the third step of the formula is where the real fun starts.

You translated your ideal routine into reality. After the initial creation of your program, you compiled it and filled any holes found in your routine. You then followed this up by debugging (or decluttering) your program.

Then, voilá! You tested your routine, and ran through it one step at a time, allowing both your body and mind to literally become programmed to do things without conscious thought.

Finally, you documented your routine and displayed it in a place that reminds you of the reason that governs your routine automation.

STANDING OVATION.

Guys.

You've done a lot.

And, the greatest part is that you can be assured that this system will continue to work.

Why?

Because this system of routine automation is based on the science of computer programming, along with the principles of decision fatigue, which have already proved to successfully contribute toward automation.

The ultra-successful and freaky productive lives of people like Steve Jobs and Mark Zuckerberg (among others who we addressed) should serve as additional evidence for you.

YOU OWE IT TO YOURSELF.

If you're reading this now and the only thing you're thinking is, "Wow, that was a good read," then your routines will never become automated.

To automate anything, including routines, a burst of work during the initial stages is required before it can run on autopilot.

Remember the dominos example from before?

There is some beginning setup, but once you pull the trigger and push the first domino over, the other dominos fall without any effort from you.

So, as a beneficiary of routine automation results, I'm here to say, "It's worth the initial upfront work, dang it."

Don't be content with just another book read.

Why?

Because here is what is possible for you when you achieve routine automation:

- You will be more productive.
- You will feel more in control of your life and circumstances.
- You, and others around you, will feel less stressed.
- You will have a clearer mind, resulting in greater creativity and spontaneity.
- You will feel more optimistic.
- And, you will exude confidence.

IF I MAY...

Here are my suggestions:

- If you haven't already, download the *Automate Your Routines, Guarantee Your Results Workbook.*
- If you haven't already, automate your morning routine.
- Follow that up by automating your evening routine, and then your eating routines.
- Then, apply the five-step formula to any other routine you need to automate.

Within three weeks (one routine per week), you will have automated three (or more) routines, consisting of hundreds of habits, habits that others try to establish their whole lives.

YOU DIDN'T THINK I'D LEAVE YOU WITHOUT A PEP TALK, DID YOU?

It *is* possible for you to automate your routines.

It *is* possible for you to preserve your willpower.

And, it *is* possible for you to use that willpower to conquer other, more meaningful things in your life.

But, solidifying the beginning and end of your day (with the occasional meal) is where you must begin.

This process is not complicated. So, don't make it!

Simply choose once (choose now!) to automate your routines, so you can automate your results.

FRIENDS DON'T LET FRIENDS NOT BE AWESOME.

Help your friends do the same!

It really is the right thing to do.

LET'S STICK TOGETHER, HEY HEY HEY.

I would love to hear about your successes and help you in any way I can.

(If you're feeling awkward about reaching out to me, refer back to the time when I told you that I was basically addicted to eating sidewalk chalk. So...yeah. We're at that level.)

Don't be a stranger.

Your fan,
Kathryn
www.booksbykathryn.com

173

AN URGENT PLEA + THANK YOU? (YES, THE QUESTION MARK IS INTENTIONAL)

(WARNING: coming up is a shameless plug for an honest Amazon review, masked in a few paragraphs of entertaining copy.)

Why am I questioning my thanks towards you?

Simply because I am not sure to what degree I should thank you.

I should probably just pledge my unborn child to you.

You know, just to be safe.

I definitely want to thank you for purchasing and reading **Automate Your Routines, Guarantee Your Results.** You could have picked from a lot of books. But, you didn't.

THANK YOU.

If you've even considered leaving an honest review on Amazon so I can provide even better solutions for you, then that definitely solicits an additional, and well deserved "thank you."

THANK YOU.

If you've actually left a review, then, wow. That requires more than a "thank you."

But, considering the chances that you and I probably aren't anywhere close to being in the same physical vicinity, kissing you on the mouth (which was my initial thought) probably isn't a possibility.

Too forward?

Okay, I've digressed.

What I meant to say was "thank you."

THANK YOU? THANK YOU. THANK YOU!

Please leave an honest review on Amazon.

SELF-PUBLISHING
SCHOOL

Don't be one of those "I'm going to write a book one day" type of people.

Instead, be one of those "I already wrote a bestseller" type of people.   (Way cooler.)

Here's a fun fact for you: I've spent tens of thousands of dollars on online courses.

Here's another fun fact: Investing in *Self-Publishing School,* the course that helped me go from zero book idea to published (in just three months), was some of the best money I've ever spent.

Want to know why else *Self-Publishing School* is so rad?

They offer an extremely comprehensive free video series.

Yes.

Free.

So, even if you're busy, bad at writing, or don't know where to start, you can write a bestseller and build your best life.

With tools and experience across a variety niches and professions, *Self-Publishing School* really is the only resource you need to take your book to the finish line.

SO, THE QUESTION IS: WHAT ARE YOU WAITING FOR?!

Watch this *free video series* now, and say "yes" to being a bestselling author.

(Seriously - *do it.*)

To access your free video training, visit
http://www.booksbykathryn.com/bestseller